Poets of the Tamil Anthologies

Princeton Library
of Asian Translations

Poets of the Tamil Anthologies

Ancient Poems of Love and War

GEORGE L. HART, III

PRINCETON UNIVERSITY PRESS
Princeton, New Jersey

Published by Princeton University Press, Princeton, New Jersey
In the United Kingdom: Princeton University Press, Guildford, Surrey

Library of Congress Cataloging in Publication Data will be
found on the last printed page of this book

Publication of this book has been aided by
the Lacy Lockert Fund of Princeton University Press

This book has been composed in VIP Bembo

Clothbound editions of Princeton University Press books
are printed on acid-free paper, and binding materials are
chosen for strength and durability.

Printed in the United States of America by
Princeton University Press, Princeton, New Jersey

For my Parents

PREFACE

While I was preparing the final manuscript of this book, I came to know and work with Hank Heifetz, a poet and novelist. Hank was kind enough to spend a large amount of time going over every poem of this translation. Not only did he help me to improve virtually every poem included here; he also persuaded me to cut the manuscript from 315 to 186 pages, an act that has made it much more readable. I can only express my gratitude to Hank for his help, for the many things he has taught me, and, above all, for his friendship, which has been a great joy to me. I am also grateful to Daniel Ingalls, who suggested that I prepare this book. I have been helped immeasurably by A. K. Ramanujan, who was not only my first Tamil teacher, but who has provided invaluable insights and suggestions. I would like also to thank Jeff Masson, who wrote a valuable criticism of the first version of this manuscript, my Tamil teacher in India, Ramasubramaniam, with whom I read and made rough translations of most of the material contained here, and my wife, Kausalya, who made many useful suggestions. I am also indebted to the University of Wisconsin, which supported me for two summers during which I worked on this book.

CONTENTS

Preface	vii
Introduction	3
Aiñkuṟunūṟu	17
Kuṟuntokai	45
Naṟṟiṇai	89
Akanāṉūṟu	107
Puṟanāṉūṟu	137

Poets of the Tamil Anthologies

INTRODUCTION

The literature of the Tamils, a people numbering about fifty million who inhabit the southeasternmost part of India as well as the north and east of Ceylon, goes back nearly two thousand years. The first literature we have in the language, written between the first and third centuries A.D., is divided into eight anthologies. The earliest five of these have provided the poems translated in this book.

The poems are divided into two great categories: *akam*, or interior, poems that view life from inside the family and concern the love between man and woman, and *puṟam*, or exterior, poems that view life from outside the family and concern such topics as kings, heroism in battle, ethics, and the life of wandering bards and poets. The techniques as well as the content of these two groups are different. *Akam* poems tend to hinge around one or more images, exploiting the complex suggestion of these images to the full. Each *akam* poem, moreover, is placed in the mouth of one of the lovers or of another character involved in the situation, which is conventional and known to the readers. *Puṟam* poems, on the other hand, are more straightforward, making less use of images and of their suggestion, and more use of simple description. Indeed, the labels of these two great categories, "inner" and "outer," could apply to the techniques of the poems themselves. *Akam* poems are introspective; each needs to be thought about in order to discover its many uses of suggestion. *Puṟam* poems are meant to be declaimed, and do not often contain suggestive metaphors whose meaning unfolds slowly. The first half of the poems translated here are *akam* poems, the second (those from the *Puṟanāṉūṟu*), *puṟam*.

Though these poems date from about the first three centuries A.D., they are modeled on oral poems, whose tradition must be much older than that. Before writing came to Tamilnad, drummers and singers existed who were of low caste and who lived by certain ritual occupations. Among the most important of their functions was to sing of the king and enhance his sacred power by their songs of praise. The singers would be employed by men of high position, to live in their houses and to entertain the occupants with songs that would lend an auspicious aura to the house and to the pastimes of the inhabitants.

In about the third century B.C., writing reached Tamilnad from North India. In the next centuries, a class of literate and learned men arose who associated themselves with the courts of kings and who composed poems. Unlike the bards and drummers, these men were for the most part of high status. However, when they fashioned poems, they used the only model at hand: the oral poetry of the low-class bards and drummers around them. Their poems are thus undoubtedly quite similar to the oral compositions of the bards (none of which has survived), and are occasionally even placed in the mouths of such bards. Sometimes, even kings became poets and composed songs. More commonly, poets became the intimate friends of kings or their advisors and wrote poems describing their friendship and giving advice.

The life of the poets of ancient Tamilnad was often not an easy one. Many of them lived from hand to mouth, not knowing where their next meal was coming from (Puṟanāṉūṟu 159, 160). The society that they lived in was unstable and warlike, for it was made up of many small kingdoms that were constantly fighting. Even the three great kings, the Chera, Chola, and Pandya, did not have much security and might be attacked and overthrown at any moment. The poets, being associated with kings, lived lives filled with danger (Puṟanāṉūṟu 47) and uncertainty (see the notes on Puṟanāṉūṟu 107). Those unable to find a royal patron were reduced to wandering from the court of one king to another and virtually begging for support (Puṟanāṉūṟu 159). It is not strange, then, that the poems of these early Tamil poets are not the rarefied, otherworldly pieces produced by the great Sanskrit poets, who lived for the most part in more secure circumstances. Rather, in the *puṟam* poems, poets write of the difficulties of everyday life and of their suffering. And even when they write *akam* poems, which are impersonal, they write with a directness and a feeling of concrete experience that is very moving.

While it is true that the poems have oral models, their conventions are quite complex. Both great categories have been divided by the commentators into seven *tiṇais*, or divisions. Each of these is named after a flower, which also gave its name to the *paṇ*, or *rāga*, in which it was sung. For the *puṟam* poems, the *tiṇais* are *veṭci*, the cattle raid; *vañci*, preparation for war and invasion; *uḻiñai*, siege; *tumpai*, battle; *vākai*, victory; *kāñci*, tragedy and the evanescent nature of life; and *pāṭāṇ*, praise. For *puṟam*, these divisions are not, in my opinion, of much consequence; they do not aid the reader in appreciating the poem in any significant way.

The case is quite different, however, for *akam*, for the *tiṇais* of that genre are encoded with a mood and a situation. The commentators list seven *tiṇais* for *akam*, but two of them are not found in the oldest anthologies and therefore are not treated here. In addition to the plant that gives it its name, each of the five *akam tiṇais* is associated with a tract of land (in which the plant is found), certain flora and fauna found in the tract, the people who live in the tract, a season, a time of day, and a situation in the development or fulfillment of love between man and woman. By invoking any of the material associated with a *tiṇai*, the poet is able to evoke the mood and situation with which it is associated in the minds of his readers, at least in theory. In fact, it is not uncommon for two or more *tiṇais* to be mixed in one poem, and the *tiṇais* are not as discrete as the commentators would like them to be. Nevertheless, the poets do use the *tiṇais* and their conventions to achieve poetic effect, and it is important to be acquainted with them. I have described the five *tiṇais* below in an order roughly corresponding to the development of love between man and woman.

1. *Kuṟiñci*. The subject is usually the secret meeting of the lovers, which may take place while the heroine guards the millet crop from birds, or at night, when the heroine must slip out of the house, evading her mother, who has begun to suspect that her daughter is up to mischief. The place is the mountains.

2. *Neytal*. The subject is often separation, during which the unmarried woman believes that her lover has abandoned her. Occasionally *neytal* poems concern the journey of the hero along the beach in his chariot as he comes to see his beloved. The place is the seashore.

3. *Pālai*. The hero sets out across the wilderness to elope with his beloved (whose parents will not give her permission to marry), or, if he is unaccompanied, to make enough money to marry her on his return (presumably by giving it as bride price). Occasionally the hero is married and undertakes a journey for business purposes, or for some god. The commentators say that, of the five *tiṇais*, *pālai* is the only one that has no specific tract, but most of the poems describe a wilderness that is dry and has a few trees. The time is midday, and the season is summer.

4. *Mullai*. The heroine, who may be married, waits for her lover to

return from a journey. Some poems in this category describe union. All concern the fertility of the rainy season in forest meadows. The time is usually evening.

5. *Marutam*. After marriage, and usually after the couple has a son, the hero leaves his wife and begins to live with courtesans. The place is the riverine tract, always the center of South Indian civilization, with its rich towns and cities supported by paddy farming. The time is day.

As one comes to know this literature, one associates a mood with each of these categories. Such associations must have been even stronger for the ancient Tamils than for the modern reader, as each of the *tiṇais* was sung in its own *rāga*, or musical mode. Below, I have given an example of each *tiṇai*, together with a description of the mood which it conveys for me.

In *kuṟiñci*, the feeling is one of mystery. The Tamils were and are an agricultural people, and for them fertility is the most important aspect of human existence. In *kuṟiñci*, the most important human relation—that between man and woman with its promise of offspring—has been initiated, but has not yet been controlled and ordered by marriage. Thus the secret union of the *kuṟiñci* poem is pervaded by a sense of imminent danger: if the heroine is unable to marry her lover, she will be considered spoiled and will be unable to marry anyone. In the majority of poems, a secret meeting takes place at night, a time when the world is silent and when dangerous powers are abroad. An example is Kuṟuntokai 47, in which the heroine thinks of her lover, journeying to meet her:

> Flowers have fallen from black-stalked *vēṅkai* trees
> onto round stones
> so they seem tiger cubs in the forest
> where he comes at night
> to do what he should not.
> Better that you were not here,
> O long white light of the moon.

Not all *kuṟiñci* poems are as mysterious as this one. Many simply celebrate the wonder of love (Aiṅkuṟunūṟu 299) or describe the change in a woman's condition after she has fallen in love (Aiṅkuṟunūṟu 216). But in all of the poems there is a sense of wonder: the union of a man and woman has been initiated.

Neytal is the least developed of the five *tiṇais*, and in it there are found several diverse situations. The most common mood, however, is despair: a woman has given herself to a man, and unless he marries her she is ruined. In many poems the man has abandoned her, leaving her alone. Often, she is distraught because of the gossip about her affair with a man who does not seem to care for her, as in Kuṟuntokai 97:

I am here.
My innocence is in the sea grove, gone,
and the pain never ends.
The shore man is in his town
and our secret is common gossip
in public places.

There are also many *neytal* poems that describe the meeting of the still unmarried hero and his beloved in much the same terms as *kuṟiñci* poems (Aiṅkuṟunūṟu 101, Kuṟuntokai 123).

In *pālai*, man seems to be fighting against nature in its most infertile manifestation as the hero, sometimes accompanied by his beloved, travels through the bone-dry wilderness that is filled with thieves and other hazards. An example is Kuṟuntokai 16:

Has he forgotten me, friend?
Like the scraping sound
when thieves turn against their nails
iron-tipped arrows to make them ready,
a red-legged lizard calls its mate
in the wilderness
filled with lovely-stemmed *kaḷḷi*
where he has gone.

Much of the effect of this poem comes from the fact that the calling of the lizard was (and is) considered auspicious.

The mood of *mullai* is one of fertility, mirrored by the greening of the woodland meadows in the monsoon after the summer. Some poems celebrate union between man and woman (Aiṅkuṟunūṟu 411); others describe the despair of the heroine, separated from her lover when all that surrounds her reminds her of union, as in Aiṅkuṟunūṟu 476, where she addresses the bard sent by the absent hero to assure her that he will soon return from his journey:

The sky covered with clouds and lightning roars
resplendent with the monsoon.
Green jasmine creepers blossom with the season
and herders with many cattle
weave them into garlands of flowers and leaves.

Tell me, unfeeling bard,
does the land where he has gone
have such loveless evenings?

Marutam poems are pervaded by a feeling of worldliness and realism. The emotional and transfiguring love of the couple before and immediately after marriage has mellowed into a more commonplace relationship. The man, tired of his wife, has begun to see courtesans, accomplished women who must have been far more interesting to talk to than the majority of high-class Tamil women, who were scarcely allowed out of their homes after puberty. The woman still loves her husband—indeed, the society left her no alternative; but her love is of a more realistic sort than the mysterious love of the *kuṟiñci* poems, and she is not above being angry with her husband. For example, in Aiṅkuṟunūṟu 84, the heroine's friend addresses the errant husband:

Even if it comes to her ears,
her anger is beyond words.
What, then, if she sees with her eyes:
like a cool pond in the winter month of Tai
played in by women with flower-fragrant hair,
your chest belongs to whores
who kiss and bathe in it.

Each *akam* poem is uttered by some person involved in its situation. These include the hero, the heroine, the heroine's real mother, the heroine's foster mother, the heroine's female friend (who may be the daughter of the foster mother), the hero's male friend, the hero's bard (who serves as a messenger for the parted couple), onlookers who see the couple eloping, neighbors, the courtesan, and the courtesan's female friend. Curiously, the girl's father and the boy's relatives do not narrate any of the poems.

Some of the suggestiveness of the imagery used in the poems will inevitably escape the western reader, who does not know much of the culture of the ancient Tamils. I have attempted to correct this situation in the notes. In this introduction, however, it seems appropriate to discuss a few of the poems and their use of imagery.

Most of the Tamil images are natural objects or phenomena that evoke fertility in some way. A simple example is Kuṟuntokai 40:

My mother and yours,
what were they to each other?
My father and yours,

how were they kin?
I and you,
how do we know each other?
And yet
like water that has rained on red fields,
our hearts in their love
have mixed together.

The union of the male rain and the female earth produces the fertility of the earth, just as the union of man and woman leads to the woman's having children, whose importance to the Tamils is indicated by Puṟanāṉūṟu 188. The movement of this poem is well constructed. It begins with "my" and "yours," progresses to "I and you," and ends with "together."

In Kuṟuntokai 25, a heron evokes a more complex suggestion. The heroine describes the day that her lover joined with her:

There was no one there,
only that man
who is like a thief.
If he lies, what can I do?
With little green legs like millet stalks,
a heron searched for eels in the running water
when he took me.

The heron, indifferent and selfish, is contrasted with the heroine, who gives herself to her lover. First of all, the heron is meant to be likened to the world. While the heroine gives herself to her lover, the world is concerned only with finding something to eat in order to stay alive. The world's only concern with the heroine's love is to gossip about it. The heron is also meant to be likened to the hero, who shares the selfish attitude of the world. The heron's eating eels from the running water is a symbol for sexual gratification: like the heron, the hero is concerned with gratifying himself, not with love and its responsibilities. In the sexual act with her lover and as the object of gossip afterwards, the heroine is as helpless as a wriggling eel in the beak of the heron. The bird's legs are like millet stems. The millet stem holds grain, the source of life for others and the fruit of fertility, while the heron's legs hold a bird that is predatory, that uses others but contributes nothing to their welfare. While it seems that the hero's act might lead to marriage with its fruit (children), it is in fact only a predatory act, and the hero has no intention of marrying his new mistress.

In Naṟṟiṇai 7, a natural tableau corresponds to the state of the lovers. The hero has set off to gain wealth without marrying his beloved. He has promised to return by the monsoon, a time when traveling is difficult. Here, the heroine's friend points out to her that the monsoon has arrived and that her lover will certainly come soon:

> The springs on wide, demon-haunted plateaus
> will overflow.
> From mountainsides waterfalls
> will roar.
> So swift it sweeps along stones,
> a forest river will descend,
> and a flood will surge
> too deep for poles
> over the barrenness.
> The clouds roar out with their voices shaking,
> lightning flashes.
> The rains are here, friend,
> to pour down on this great, dry barrenness,
> with its sandal trees with tiny leaves
> and its slopes thick with pepper,
> where huge elephants eat white millet seeds
> and sleep.

The contrast is between two states of mind symbolized by two seasons. In one, the heroine is without her lover and her state is as arid as the woodland in the dry season. In that landscape, even small indications of green, like the tiny leaves of the sandal trees, are notable. Elephants survive on white millet seeds, an unnatural food for them, because there is nothing else for them to eat. After they eat, they have nothing to do but sleep. Like the elephants, the heroine cannot have the nourishment that is natural to her, but must exist with frustrating memories. Nor does she have anything to do. But when her lover has come, things will be different. Just as the forest is covered by water that flows from sacred slopes in the rainy season, she will be absorbed in the bliss of union, whose ultimate source is otherworldly. Just as the fertility of the earth is the result of water falling on fields, the union of man and woman is necessary for human fertility. When such union takes place, ecstasy is so overpowering that it cannot be controlled, just as the water is so deep that poles cannot be used to guide boats on it. The poem is made more effective by the changing visual focus of the imagery. It begins with the overflowing of sacred springs, continues with the waterfalls and the river, and reaches the plains. Then it goes up to the sky and the cloud, and then returns to a very different earth, parched and infertile.

In Kuṟuntokai 104 the grazing of cattle and the falling of raindrops are likened to the state of a woman parted from her lover. She remembers the day that he left her to go in search of wealth:

> Friend, listen.
> Like pearls when their string is cut,
> cool drops came down
> and cattle grazed at dawn
> on cold, thick bindweed
> in the mist
> the day my lover left.
> Since then
> there have been many days alone.

The falling dew and the grazing cattle are images of fertility, suggesting the sexual bliss of the united couple. But the image of fertility is contradicted by the cold and by the time of the day (dawn), when the bliss of union comes to an end and more mundane occupations take up men's time. The pearls, to which the falling drops are likened, are meant to be compared to the days that have passed since the hero left. Just as pearls fall without order or connection when the string connecting them is cut, so the days have passed with nothing to relate one to the next, without any coherence. When pearls are strung together to form a necklace, they make an ornament that women wear to signify their auspicious state—that they are not widowed, and that their husband is at home. Should he die or go on a journey, they are not supposed to wear ornaments. The ruined pearl necklace described in this poem suggests the very perilous state of the heroine, who does not even know whether her husband is alive, and who cannot wear ornaments until he returns.

In Puṟanāṉūṟu 255 a mountain and its shade symbolize a state of release from worldly problems and, ultimately, death. A wife stands over the body of her dead husband (who presumably has been killed in battle) and cries out:

> I would cry out for help, but I am afraid of tigers.
> I would embrace you, but I cannot lift your broad chest.
> May evil Death, who made you suffer so,
> shiver as I do.

Take my wrist, thick with bangles,
and we will reach the shade of the mountain.
Come, walk, it is very near.

If the wife cries out for help, tigers may come; if she seeks aid, those to whom she goes for refuge will abuse her and take advantage of her. The word for help, *aiyō*, is also a cry expressing suffering or despair. If the wife even attempts to express her grief, misfortune will come. Unable to express her suffering, she wishes to embrace her husband, but she lacks the strength even to do that. Utterly frustrated, and unable to receive aid either from the outside world or from her husband, she tries to vent her grief by making another suffer: she curses Death, but Death can feel no pain. Finally, she wishes to take her husband where the hot sun will not burn him: she would go to the shadow of the mountain with him. The sun, which can be brutally hot in South India, is often used in these poems as a symbol for the suffering of worldly life. Here the wife means that she would leave the suffering of this life and go to the peace of death with her husband. She asks him to take her wrist, thick with bangles, a sign that she is not a widow, and walk with her, but he cannot. She may die, but death is not the same as going to the other world of peace and rest with her husband. The ancient Tamils believed that widows were possessed by a dangerous sacred power that rendered them hazardous to all and that could be contained only by severe asceticism or by suicide (*suttee*). This state is mirrored in this poem: the wife is cut off from the world and her only concern is her husband's body, which she would protect from the sun and from tigers. She is obsessed by death and no longer belongs to this world.

In addition to imagery such as that analyzed in the above poems, the ancient Tamils, like all poets, relied upon rhythm and sound to achieve effect. Such devices are, of course, impossible to reproduce in translation, though the translator may try to recreate them in his own language. To give some idea of the use of sound and rhythm in the original, I should like to analyze one poem in some detail.

In Kuṟuntokai 234, the heroine expresses her grief, as she is separated from her lover:

The sun goes down and the sky reddens, pain grows sharp,
light dwindles. Then is evening
when jasmine flowers open, the deluded say.
But evening is the great brightening dawn

when crested cocks crow all through the tall city
and evening is the whole day
for those without their lovers.

A literal word-for-word rendering is as follows, with hyphenated phrases representing one word in Tamil:

> Sun going sky as-it-reddens, pain having-sharpened,
> light cutting-off time-of jasmine flowering
> evening they-say, they-who-are-deluded.
> Crest cock[s] tall city crying
> great brightening dawn-also evening,
> day-also evening, help for-those-without.

Tamil is a highly agglutinative language in which relationships are quite clear, even if they are less defined than in English. There would be little question, on the part of someone versed in Tamil, regarding the grammatical structure and meaning of this verse. Nevertheless, it is quite evident that Tamil does not tie down words as specifically as English does. The result of this, I believe, is that poetry in Tamil is more conducive to the play of suggestion than English poetry, or Sanskrit.

This poem is an excellent example of the metrical and alliterative techniques which the poets used. Tamil meter—at least the meter used in the poems translated here—is on the surface quite simple. It is based on length, like Latin and Greek meters; however, unlike most meters in those languages, it is quantitative, not syllabic. Each line is divided into four feet (though the penultimate line may have three feet), and each foot must contain one of the combinations of the equivalent of four short syllables given below:

˘ ˘ ˘ ˘
– ˘ ˘
˘ ˘ –
– –

A foot may also consist of the equivalent of six short syllables, in which case it must have one of the above configurations plus a long syllable.

In general, Tamil rhyme consists of alliteration between the same part of two different feet. Often it is the beginning part of the feet which is rhymed, or two feet at the beginning of lines. Thus Tamil is said to have beginning rhyme (though end rhyme is also encountered).

In later Tamil verse, beginning rhyme becomes far more common and more complete. In the following analysis, Kuṟ. 234 is broken into metrical units, and rhyming portions are underlined. It should be pointed out that in many places in a foot, length or shortness may be made by position.

Cuṭarcel / vāṉañ / ceppap / paṭarkūrn /
tellaṟu / poḻutiṉ / mullai / malarum /
mālai / yeṉmaṉār / mayaṅki / yōrē /
kuṭumik / kōḻi / neṭunaka / riyampum /
perumpular / viṭiyalu / mālai /
pakalu / mālai / tuṇaiyi / lōrkkē / .

Of course, there is more alliteration than this strictly formal analysis indicates; for example, the word *mālai* occurs twice in the last two lines, with obvious alliteration. In terms of meter, the poem goes at a stately pace until the fourth line, when it suddenly becomes rapid and full of short syllables. This corresponds to a change in subject to dawn, a time of awakening and action. Similarly, the alliteration in the poem is subdued, with full liquid and nasal sounds until the fourth line, when the mood is suddenly changed by the introduction of k's and p's. Then, as the subject matter reverts to evening, the poem modulates, and in the last half of the fifth line and the final line, the meter is once again stately, while the liquids and nasals return. The imagery of the poem also corresponds to the mood and to the prosody. In the beginning, the poem describes mellow, soft objects: the reddening sun, dwindling rays, flowering jasmine. Then suddenly in the fourth line, with the change of scene to dawn, the imagery becomes harsh, pointed, and active: crested cocks in a tall city, the brightening dawn, when the sun is growing brighter. Finally, the poem modulates back to evening and separation.

The anthologies from which the poems in this book have been chosen include four collections of *akam* poems, the *Aiṅkuṟunūṟu*, the *Kuṟuntokai*, the *Naṟṟiṇai*, and the *Akanāṉūṟu*, and one collection of *puṟam* poems, the *Puṟanāṉūṟu*. The *Aiṅkuṟunūṟu*, or "five hundred short poems," consists of 500 poems of from three to five lines by five poets. Each hundred treats one *tiṇai* of *akam*. The *Kuṟuntokai*, or "anthology of short poems," contains 401 poems of from six to eight lines by 205 poets, arranged without regard to *tiṇai*. The *Naṟṟiṇai*, or "good *tiṇai*," contains four hundred poems of from nine to twelve lines by 192 poets, also arranged without regard to *tiṇai*. The *Akanāṉūṟu*, or "four hundred *akam* poems," contains four hundred poems of from thirteen to thirty-one lines by 142 poets, arranged in such a way that odd-numbered poems are *pālai*, poems ending in -2 and -8 are *kuṟiñci*, poems ending in -4 are *mullai*, poems ending in -6 are *marutam*, and poems ending in -0 are *neytal*. I have given the *tiṇai* of poems from the *Aiṅkuṟunūṟu* and from the *Akanāṉūṟu*, since those anthologies specify the *tiṇai* of each poem. Since the other two *akam* anthologies do not give this information, I have omitted it, as any attribution on my part would be arbitrary.

The *Puṟanāṉūṟu*, or "four hundred *puṟam* poems," contains four hundred poems of between four and forty lines by 156 poets. They are arranged roughly by topic according to the following scheme (which applies to this selection, not to all the poems of the *Puṟanāṉūṟu*):

Poem number	*Subject matter*
19-52	The praise of kings (except 47).
47	A request made of a king by a poet.
65	On the death of a king.
74	A poem written by a king.
77-165	Poems by poets to their royal patrons.
182-193	Poems on ethical or philosophical themes.
213-300	Poems on death and tragedy.
213-223	On the death by suicide of Kōpperuñcōḻaṉ (see the notes on 213).
228-238	Poems mourning the death of kings.
243	On old age.
245	On the death of a king's wife.
248	On the death of a king.
255-281	On women and the death of their men in battle.
300	On a man seeking revenge for the killing of his brother.
305	On the role of an envoy in ending a war.
316	On a fighting man.
349-350	Poems on a girl who is the cause of fighting.
356-364	General poems on death and tragedy.

All of the poems are accompanied by a colophon, a short statement of the situation of the poem that must have been composed long after the poems themselves. For the *akam* poems, the colophon is usually superfluous and sometimes undesirable, placing unnecessary restrictions on the poem. I have therefore omitted it, though I have supplied its information in the notes where necessary. In the poems of the *Puṟanāṉūṟu*, on the other hand, the colophon gives valuable information about the author of the poem, the king sung, and the circumstances under which the poem was composed. I have therefore included it.

I have made this introduction as brief as possible, giving only the most basic information about the poems. Those readers who are interested in discovering more about the poems, their techniques, their conventions, and the society from which they came, can consult some of the books and articles given in the bibliography. I would especially draw the reader's attention to two books written entirely about the anthologies: *Heroic Tamil Poetry* (London, Oxford University Press, 1968), by K. Kailasapathy, and *The Poems of Ancient Tamil: Their Milieu and Their Sanskrit Counterparts* (Berkeley, University of California Press, 1975), by me.

The poems of the Tamil anthologies, of which I have here given a small but representative selection, have for me a significance that far transcends what, at first glance, is their somewhat limited subject matter. The love poems take one small event, one image that seems trivial, and with that material describe an intense human experience in a sudden and wonderful way, creating in a few words a richness of suggestion and feeling that resonates in the reader's mind long afterward. The war poems contrast the demands of society with human needs, pointing out a dilemma that is the source of most tragedy. As the poems take up these issues—how a person may experience, how he may exist with the unfeeling conventions and demands of society—they offer no simple answers. What they do is to consider them with a complexity and profundity that seems inexhaustible, a continual source of insight and pleasure. In many ways, they fit what the poet Kapilar is supposed to have written about the ethical work called the *Tirukkuṟaḷ*. Even more than the verses of that book, perhaps, each of these poems might be likened to

> a drop, smaller than a millet grain,
> hanging on a tiny blade of grass
> and mirroring the greatness of a towering palmyra tree.

Aiñkur̲unūr̲u

Aiñkuṟunūṟu 24

Spotted crabs whose mothers die bearing them
and crocodiles that eat their young
live in his town.
Has he come now?
Why does he embrace women
so their gold bangles jingle,
use up their loveliness,
and leave?

Marutam
Ōrampōkiyār

Aiṅkuṟunūṟu 35

It used to be more radiant
than the color of the soft peeled stalk
of a waterlily in the pond of our town,
but now
my dark skin has become pale.

Marutam
Ōrampōkiyār

Aiṅkuṟunūṟu 74

Her bright ornaments of fresh gold gently radiant,
she climbed the *marutam* tree on the bank
and plunged into the water,
and her cool, fragrant hair
was as splendid as a peacock descending from the sky

Marutam
Ōrampōkiyār

Aiṅkuṟunūṟu 84

Even if it comes to her ears,
her anger is beyond words.
What, then, if she sees with her eyes:
like a cool pond in the winter month of Tai
played in by women with flower-fragrant hair,
your chest belongs to whores
who kiss and bathe in it.

Marutam
Ōrampōkiyār

Aiñkuṟunūṟu 101

Look there, mother.
Cutting the long vines of the green *aṭampu*
as it goes up and down
and crushing dark waterlilies,
the chariot has come,
driven by the man from the seashore
who is remedy for the grief
that has come to your daughter's flowerlike eyes

Neytal
Ammūvaṉār

Aiñkuṟunūṟu 113

Yesterday, friend, some people of this town said
that I am the woman of him
whose bay has high waves that break the white sand.
Mother heard and asked,
"Is it you?"
and I answered very softly,
"Yes."

Neytal
Ammūvaṉār

Aiṅkuṟunūṟu 146

My black loveliness is sweet
for the man from a bay
where ripening clusters of buds
opening on the *ñāḻal* bush on the dune
smell fragrant.

Neytal
Ammūvaṉār

Aiṅkuṟunūṟu 177

Even though they have done no wrong,
they will surely tremble
who have known the arms
of her who is like Toṇṭi city,
redolent with the fragrant flowers of nightshade
on tall dunes of heaped sand
shifting under rolling waves.

Neytal
Ammūvaṉār

Aiñkuṟunūṟu 197

Her bangles jingling,
she stood kicking at a crab,
her head lowered,
her face hidden by her hair.
But as soon as evening with its loneliness has gone,
she will give me her breasts
with all their loveliness.

Neytal
Ammūvaṉār

Aiṅkuṟunūṟu 203

Listen, friend,
sweeter than milk mixed with the honey from our garden
is the muddy water
that animals drink and leave
in leaf-covered holes in his land.

Kuṟiñci
Kapilar

Aiñkuṟunūṟu 206

Look there, friend!
He stands like a sentinel of this rainy hill,
his glistening, garland-like sword wet with drops,
his big anklets covered with moss,
his striped belt drenched by the cold.

Kuṟiñci
Kapilar

[The heroine's friend tells her that her lover waits to meet her outside at night.]

Aiñkuṟunūṟu 208

Mother, listen:
the deep holes that forest men dig for tubers
are filled with golden *vēṅkai* flowers
in his land.
Whenever his high mountain, colored blue-sapphire, disappeared in the
evening,
her long eyes like cut flowers
filled with gold.

Kuṟiñci
Kapilar

[*Vēṅkai* flowers are white, with a small tip of yellow. They do not last long, but fall leaving a lovely whitish-yellow carpet beneath the tree. In Tamil, the *vēṅkai* is often compared to a tiger because of the similarity in color. The gold covering the heroine's eyes is paleness.]

Aiṅkuṟunūṟu 295

My heart has gone with him.
Will it come back,
or will it stay with him
where it wants to be?
On his mountain,
peacocks flee from the torches of hill men
and terrify little birds in the stubble of the grain field,
running like girls playing ball.

Kuṟiñci
Kapilar

[Since the grain has been cut, the heroine no longer goes out to guard it from birds and cannot meet her lover as she keeps watch over the field.]

Aiñkuṟunūṟu 299

Even the dark waterlily
with its mouth opening wide
as it blooms in the fresh spring
on the slope of the hill man
cannot bloom
like the eyes of the mountain girl
with a swaying walk and gleaming, fine hair.
Even the peacock
cannot be as lovely
as she.

Kuṟiñci
Kapilar

Aiñkuṟunūṟu 320

He has gone into a fearful wilderness
where roads are forked
and where on thorny-trunked red cotton trees
bunches of large bright flowers
are caught by the roaring, fiery wind
and drop on the black earth
like the fire that falls with thunder.
He has given me a sickness
that will not go away.

Pālai
Ōtalāntaiyār

Aiṅkuṟunūṟu 331

Friend, the way he went is cruel, they say.
In that hard mountain land
bunches of white flowers unfurl
and hang on black-branched *marā* trees,
smelling so sweet
that travelers remember those they have left at home

Pālai
Ōtalāntaiyār

Aiṅkuṟunūṟu 341

He does not come,
but the season is at hand
when the cuckoo calls in a sweet voice
and tiny rivulets of water
tremble by black sand.

Pālai
Ōtalāntaiyār

Aiṅkuṟunūṟu 388

If you sit in the striped shade of the black-trunked *yā* tree
until the hot rage of the blazing sun has calmed
and then cross over the little hill,
you will see the wasteland
the youth crossed into with a conquering spear
with the girl whose body is like gold,
whose bangles are dense on her arms.

Pālai
Ōtalāntaiyār

[This poem is addressed to the foster mother of the heroine, who has eloped with her lover.]

Aiṅkuṟunūṟu 393

You grow thin grieving because she left,
and, your eyes filled with tears,
you speak out against the injustice of the world.
But see,
your daughter has come back to comfort your troubled heart
with the brave youth
who carries a conquering spear.

Pālai
Ōtalāntaiyār

[This poem is addressed to the mother of the heroine, who eloped and is now returning.]

Aiṅkuṟunūṟu 405

Like the red flame shining in the bowl of a lamp,
she has become the light of her house,
for she bore his son
whose land is ornamented with meadows
grown lovely with flowers in the pattering rain.

Mullai
Pēyaṉār

Aiṅkuṟunūṟu 411

With drops splattering
as they fall from the loud-voiced clouds,
the rains have started on the lovely meadows.
We will play in the new water
that brings desire.
You whose hair is long and dark, come quickly

Mullai
Pēyaṉār

Aiṅkuṟunūṟu 431

The way your lover went
is beautiful.
On large hills with lovely colors,
peacocks have forms
colored blue sapphire.

Mullai
Pēyaṉār

[The friend consoles the heroine, saying that the land her lover entered to find wealth is not a dangerous wilderness, but a land of fertility.]

Aiñkuṟunūṟu 437

The way your lover went
is beautiful.
In the cool rain and hail,
jasmine blooms white.

Mullai
Pēyaṉār

[See the notes on Aiñkuṟunūṟu 431.]

Aiṅkuṟunūṟu 476

The sky covered with clouds and lightning roars
resplendent with the monsoon.
Green jasmine creepers blossom with the season
and herders with many cattle
weave them into garlands of flowers and leaves.
Tell me, unfeeling bard,
does the land where he has gone
have such loveless evenings?

Mullai
Pēyaṉār

[The hero, absent on business, has sent his bard to assure the heroine that he has not forgotten her and will return.]

Aiṅkuṟunūṟu 479

Tell me, bard who make all your words so sweet.
I have crossed many lands
and now every day
the merciless northwind with its unrelenting cold
mocks my loneliness.
Tell what she,
her eyes cold flowers,
said for me.

Mullai
Pēyaṉār

[The bard, sent by the heroine, comes with a message from her to her husband, who is away from home.]

Kuṟuntokai

Kuṟuntokai 1

Making the field red with his killing
he crushes demons.
He has red-shafted arrows,
red-tusked elephants,
whirling battle anklets.
This hill belongs to Murugan
and it is thick with clusters of blood-flowered *kāntaḷ*.

Tipput Tōḷār

[The hero, wishing to make love to his woman, has brought a gift of red *kāntaḷ* flowers, whose acceptance means that she will have him. In this poem, she refuses his offering.]

Kuṟuntokai 3

Larger than earth,
higher than sky,
harder to measure than the waters
is my love for him
whose land has hillsides of black-stalked *kuṟiñci* flowers
that yield rich honey.

Tēvakkulattār

[Swaminathaier remarks, "They say that this [*kuṟiñci*] blooms once in twelve years, that the honey that bees make from its flowers is quite delicious, and that a tribe called the Totuvar [the Todas] who live in the Nilgiris reckon their ages by counting the number of times this plant has bloomed from birth."]

Kuruntokai·6

The night is half gone.
Without words,
people are calm and quiet.
Its hate gone,
this vast world also sleeps.
Only I
do not sleep.

Patumanār

[A woman grieves when her lover is away from her.]

Kuṟuntokai 7

The bowman has battle rings on his legs
and the bangled girl wears anklets on her soft feet.
They seem good people. Who are they?
They must be desperate
to approach the bamboo-thick wasteland
where white pods of *vākai* rattle as they strike together,
blown by the wind,
like the drums when Aryans dance on tightropes.

Perumpatumaṉār

[*Vākai* is also called "the woman's tongue" because its dry pods rattle incessantly in the lightest breeze. The couple described in the poem is eloping. The last line refers to North Indians, who would come to the south and make money by performing on tightropes.]

Kuṟuntokai 16

Has he forgotten me, friend?
Like the scraping sound
when thieves turn against their nails
iron-tipped arrows to make them ready,
a red-legged lizard calls its mate
in the wilderness
filled with lovely-stemmed *kaḷḷi*
where he has gone.

Pālaipāṭiya Peruṅkaṭuṅkō

[Normally, the calling of lizards was considered auspicious. *Kaḷḷi*, or milk-hedge, is a plant found in barren places.]

Kuṟuntokai 25

There was no one there,
only that man
who is *like* a *thief*.
If he lies, what can I do?
With little green legs like millet stalks,
a heron searched for eels in the running water
when he took me.

Kapilar

Kuṟuntokai 28

Shall I attack these people, shall I strike them?
I do not know.
Or shall I find some reason and cry out
to this city that sleeps
not knowing my suffering
while the moving wind swirls
and pulls me to and fro.

Auvaiyār

[This poem is spoken by the heroine.]

Kuṟuntokai 40

My mother and yours,
what were they to each other?
My father and yours,
how were they kin?
I and you,
how do we know each other?
And yet
like water that has rained on red fields,
our hearts in their love
have mixed together.

Cempulappeyanīrār

[The poet's name means "he of water that has rained on red fields." It is the custom in Tamilnad to marry one's cross-cousin.].

Kuṟuntokai 41

When my lover is near,
I am filled with joy, I exult
like a city in festival.
But like a lonely house left by its people,
a house in a little jungle village of pleasant homes
with a squirrel playing in its yard,
I grieve alone, friend,
when he is gone.

Aṇilāṭumuṉṟilār

[The poet's name means "he of the squirrel playing in the yard."]

Kuṟuntokai 42

Even if desire should cease,
man from where a great midnight rain beats down
with thunder and lightning
and makes a waterfall resound through a cave,
will the bond wear away
that links me to you?

Kapilar

Kuṟuntokai 44

My feet will not walk further.
My eyes
looking and looking
have lost their clearness.
Surely more than the stars in the wide dark sky
are strangers in this world.

Veḷḷi Vītiyār

[This poem is uttered by the foster mother, who searches for her eloped daughter in the wilderness.]

Kuṟuntokai 47

Flowers have fallen from black-stalked *vēṅkai* trees
onto round stones
so they seem tiger cubs in the forest
where he comes at night
to do what he should not.
Better that you were not here,
O long white light of the moon.

Neṭuveṇṇilaviṉār

[The heroine speaks of her lover, who is coming to meet her at night. The poet's name means "he of the long white light of the moon." *Vēṅkai* flowers are colored like tiger skins.]

Kuṟuntokai 54

I am here.
My loveliness has perished there
with the man of forests,
where a wild elephant,
frightened by the sound of slings of the millet guards,
lets loose a green stalk of bamboo
so it springs up
like a pole catching a fish.

Mīṉeṟitūṇṭilār

[The poet's name means "he of the pole springing up." The point of this poem appears to be that the hero was enjoying the heroine, just as the elephant was grazing on the green bamboo stalk. But then, frightened by the talk that began, he suddenly abandoned her, just as the elephant leaves the bamboo when startled by the noise of the slings.]

Kuṟuntokai 58

You tell me I am wrong, my friend,
that I should stop seeing her.
Yes, I know it would be good
if I could do what you say,
but my pain
is like butter melting
on a ledge scorched in the sun
while a man who has no hands or tongue
tries to save it.
It spreads through me
no matter what I do.

Veḷḷi Vītiyār

[This poem is uttered by the hero to a companion who reproaches him for taking love too seriously.]

Kuṟuntokai 95

Descending from a great hill,
a waterfall resounds in rock caves
on flowering slopes
near the small village of the mountain man,
father of a girl with rounded arms.
Her beauty gentle as water
has ruined my firelike strength.

Kapilar

Kuṟuntokai 97

I am here.
My innocence is in the sea grove, gone,
and the pain never ends.
The shore man is in his town
and our secret is common gossip
in public places.

Veṇpūti

Kuṟuntokai 104

Friend, listen.
Like pearls when their string is cut,
cool drops came down
and cattle grazed at dawn
on cold, thick bindweed
in the mist
the day my lover left.
Since then
there have been many days alone.

Kāvaṉmullaip Pūtaṉār

Kuruntokai 123

Like thickened darkness,
cool moist shadows
lie on sand as white as gathered moonlight.
With its black-branched *puṉṉai* trees
the flowering grove is empty.
Still he does not come,
but the boat draws near
of my brothers who search for fish.

Aiyūr Muṭavaṉ

[This poem is spoken by the heroine, who is waiting for her lover to come to a secret meeting.]

Kuṟuntokai 130

He will not dig up the earth and enter it,
he will not climb into the sky,
he will not walk across the dark sea.
If we search every country,
every city,
every village,
can your lover escape us?

Veḷḷi Vītiyār

[The friend speaks to the heroine about her lover, who has left on a journey and not returned.]

Kuṟuntokai 131

Her round arms are as lovely as swaying bamboo,
her large eyes are angry.
The town she lives in is far away
and my heart rushes toward her
like a farmer with one plow
when his field is wet and ready.

Ōrēruḻavaṉār

[The poet's name means "he of the farmer with one plow."]

Kuṟuntokai 161

The sun gave no light
and the rain, relentless, came down so hard
that even the eyes of demons shivered,
and mother, holding tight her son,
who wore a necklace of tiger teeth,
cried out to me.
What did my man feel, then,
as he came,
his breast fragrant with sandal from his mountain,
and stood outside like a drenched elephant?

Nakkīrar

[Because her mother is awake and watchful, the heroine is unable to keep her rendezvous with her lover.]

Kuṟuntokai 165

Like drinking past being happy,
you lusted until you could not control your desire.
Like salt being loaded into a wagon
on a shore filled with ruts
in the rain pouring down,
you were ruined
once you saw the natural loveliness
of her thick dark hair.

Paraṇar

[The hero addresses his heart.]

Kuṟuntokai 189

Today I will go
and tomorrow I will return.
My white chariot will speed like a waterfall dropping from a hill.
Its wheels,
flashing light like crescent moons,
will cut down green plants
like the fire that falls from the sky.
Going as swift as the wind,
I will come in the evening,
and when I take the fine body of my woman
with a few rows of white bangles on her wrists,
I will be happy.

Maturai Īḻattup Pūtaṉṟēvaṉ

Kuṟuntokai 220

The millet flourishing from an old rain has been harvested.
Only its stems are left,
grazed over and chewed to stubble by stags.
Jasmine blossoms like a laughing wildcat,
loosing fresh flowers from its tiny buds.
It is evening in the meadow fragrant with flowers
and bees swarm.
But see, friend,
my man who set out to find wealth
has not returned.

Okkūr Mācātti

[The first part of the poem suggests that the heroine first met her lover while she was guarding the millet from birds. The fact that the millet has now been harvested, leaving a bare field, symbolizes her state since her lover has left.]

Kuṟuntokai 224

This suffering is worse
than the pain I feel when I cannot sleep
and I remember him who left
to take long, forking paths
filled with trouble
where *yā* trees grow.
Like a voiceless man
who sees the agony
of a tawny cow fallen
into a well at night,
I cannot bear to see
the pain my friend feels for me.

Kūvaṉ Maintaṉ

[This poem is uttered by the heroine, whose lover has left to find wealth. She speaks of her friend, who tries to console her.]

Kuṟuntokai 227

Their gold rims like ornaments,
the wheels, sharp as swords,
have cut the rich petals of waterlilies
and stunted them
here in the grove where his chariot passed.

Ōta Ñāṉi

[The heroine or her friend describes the coming of the hero to the secret meeting place.]

Kuṟuntokai 231

Even though he lives in my village,
he does not come to my street.
And even if he comes
he does not hold me close.
He sees me and passes me by
as if I were a burning ground for strangers.
The desire that darkened my reason and killed my shame
has gone far off
like an arrow shot from a bow.

Pālaipāṭiya Peruñkaṭuṅkō

[The burning ground, where the dead are cremated, is the most inauspicious of places.]

Kuṟuntokai 240

Spread over cold bushes,
green bean creepers
are filled with flowers bright as parrots' beaks.
They press on jasmine flowers shaped like wildcats' teeth
in the northwind that comes,
I am filled with pain.
See, friend, like a ship sinking on the clear, wave-covered sea,
his tall hill which yields jewels
disappears in the evening.

Kollaṉ Aḻici

[The heroine sees the hill, from which her lover comes, disappear in the dusk of evening.]

Ku<u>r</u>untokai 273

Listen, you whose face is cool and fragrant
as the night wind moving
through a great forest
glistening with pollen-filled buds,
listen,
what I say can help you stop being so afraid.
The people of this world, with all their gossip,
are like a fool who climbs an old bamboo ladder
without testing it
to reach a slope where he has seen
the finest honey.
They will never have what they want,
for your man will not leave
while you and I are here.

Ciṟaikkuṭi Yāntaiyār

[The heroine's friend assures her that her lover will not leave her to search for wealth.]

Kuṟuntokai 290

"Bear your desire," they say.
Don't they know?
Or do they have such strength?
If I do not see my lover,
my heart grows thick with grief,
and like a streak of foam where a flood hits on rocks,
bit by bit I cease to be.

Kalporuciṟunuraiyār

[The poet's name means "he of the streak of foam hitting on rocks."]

Kuṟuntokai 300

Your black gathered hair is
fragrant with the dark waterlily;
your red mouth, filled with sweetness,
is redolent of the white waterlily;
and your dark body is flushed with tiny spots,
like the pollen of lotuses that flourish in deep waters.
When I tell you not to be afraid,
you should believe me,
for even if I could have the whole earth
encircled by the sea,
on whose shores geese with tiny feet sleep on heaped sands,
I would not think of giving up your love.

Ciṟaikkuṭi Yāntaiyār

[The hero assures his love that he will not leave her in search of wealth.]

Kuṟuntokai 305

The blazing fire of passion that came when I would see him
still burns to the marrow of my bones,
and yet no more do I go to him with desire
and embrace him.
And he does not come any more
to make the pain I feel go away.
Like the lonely fight of scavenger cocks
with no one to start it, no one to say when it's over,
unless it ceases of itself,
no one will free me of my pain.

Kuppaikkōḻiyār

[The scavenger cocks are contrasted with birds used in cockfights
The name of the poet means "he of the scavenger cocks."]

Kuṟuntokai 323

What are these days for?
They are only husks.
But when bards play the *rāga* of parting
so their high notes rise in the sky
and jasmine blooms across rained-on fields,
the pollen from its fresh buds
perfuming the face of my woman,
and when I sleep in her arms—
on those days I am alive.

Pataṭivaikalār

[The poet's name means "he of the days that are husks." The *rāga* of parting, *paṭumalai*, is actually one of the twelve subdivisions of the mode of *pālai*; more than that is not known. The poet's simile suggests that esthetic experience is one thing, real experience, something quite different. The hero affirms that he will not leave his beloved to travel for wealth.]

Kuṟuntokai 324

Skilled at taking their prey,
crocodiles with curving legs
keep men away from the grove-encircled waters,
yet you, in your love,
come swimming that dark backwater
with its shoals of fish.
In her innocence, she is afraid,
and I,
as if my twin children had drunk poison,
feel a terror in my heart, great lord.

Kavaimakaṉ

[The poet's name means "he of the twin children." This poem is uttered by the heroine's friend, who is frightened by the passionate love growing between the two lovers.]

Kuṟuntokai 325

"I am going, I am going," he said.
Yet even then,
I thought it was his old, empty threat and I replied,
"Go away then and don't come back."
Where is my lord, my support?
The space between my breasts
has become empty
like a great pond
where white herons
with black legs search
for prey.

Naṉṉākaiyār

Kuṟuntokai 330

The white flowers unfolding from the buds of large-leafed *pakaṉṟai*
are wrinkled
like garments dipped in the water of a cool pond
and kept wet
by a lovely washerwoman
after she has starched and beaten them.
Like strong, sweet toddy,
they smell without fragrance.
Tell me, friend,
in the land where he has gone
is the evening so empty
and lonely?

Kaḻārkkīraṉeyiṟṟiyaṉ

Kuṟuntokai 352

Their wings soft and curved
like leaf-edges of white waterlilies in deep water,
bats with sharp claws
go towards the hillside of wide-leafed jack trees
and leave the trees lonely
where they hung all day.
I learned that there are such empty, small evenings,
friend,
when I stopped seeing him.

Kaṭiyalūr Uruttiraṅkaṇṇaṉār

Kuṟuntokai 355

The rain hides everything,
and you cannot see the sky.
The water flows, spreading everywhere,
and you cannot see the earth.
The sun has gone down,
a great darkness has fallen.
You, at this midnight with everyone asleep,
how did you come, man from tall hills?
And how did you know our village,
redolent with *vēṅkai*?
I tremble in fear.

Kapilar

[*Vēṅkai* flowers, fallen on rocks, are often said to be mistaken for tigers.]

Kuṟuntokai 359

See, bard, it is a beautiful thing.
In the fresh white moonlight that spreads in the evening,
on a short-legged bed covered with fragrant flowers,
the man of victories, overcome with love,
pulls in his breath like a sleeping elephant
and embraces his son
while from behind him the mother holds him close.

Pēyaṉ

Kuṟuntokai 376

Like the sandalwood trees on the slopes of Potiyal,
where demons prowl and no living thing comes near,
she is cool in summer.
But in winter,
like the heart of a lotus
that closes to collect the slanting rays
and stores the moving sunlight,
she is warm.

Paṭumarattu Mōcik Koṟṟaṉ

Kuṟuntokai 393

The days my man embraced me,
crushing my garland of mixed flowers,
were very few,
and yet the gossip is greater than the cries of the Koṅkaṉs,
whose swords shone
the day Atikaṉ,
fighting for the Pandyan king who wears a newly made ornament,
fell with his elephant on the field of Vākai,
where male owls roam.

Paraṇar

Kuṟuntokai 399

Like the scum on the well
from which the townsfolk drink,
my paleness goes away
whenever my lover touches me.
And whenever he leaves
it spreads over me again.

Paraṇar

Naṟṟiṇai

Naṟṟiṇai 7

The springs on wide, demon-haunted plateaus
will overflow.
From mountainsides waterfalls
will roar.
So swift it sweeps along stones,
a forest river will descend,
and a flood will surge
too deep for poles
over the barrenness.
The clouds roar out with their voices shaking,
lightning flashes.
The rains are here, friend,
to pour down on this great, dry barrenness,
with its sandal trees with tiny leaves
and its slopes thick with pepper,
where huge elephants eat white millet seeds
and sleep.

Nalveḷḷiyār

[The heroine's friend points out to her that the monsoon is at hand and that her lover will soon return from his journey.]

Naṟṟiṇai 153

The cloud draws water from the eastern sea,
rises to the west growing dark
and makes the earth with its good soil bright
as lightning flashes,
colored like an urn cast of molten copper by smiths.
Everywhere the cloud rains down,
its voice sweet to the ear.
Then it goes to the south
and melts away,
like my life
now that my heart has gone to my man
and will not come back;
like my life that is left here,
as miserable
as a lone son guarding the wasteland of a great city
whose people have fled,
turned to flight by an enemy king
of raging anger who has won the battle.

Taṉimakaṉār

[The poet's name means "he of the lone son."]

Naṟṟiṇai 303

It is midnight.
Its noise stilled,
the boisterous town is quiet in sleep.
Again and again I hear
the yearning cry of the pair of *aṉṟil* birds
from their nest in the crooked spathe
of the huge-trunked palmyra in the courtyard,
a place long haunted by a god,
and my eyes do not close in sleep
and I seem to grow thin from the pain I feel.
Does he know his lovely-faced woman suffers
because of him, friend,
he from a village by the deep-water ocean,
where a killer shark roams, filled with hate
after tearing his way through a net
of curved knots and straight sticks
thrown by strong-handed fishermen in the clear sea?

Maturai Ārvalanāṭṭu Ālampēri Cāttaṉār

Naṟṟiṇai 311

When it rains,
our town is prosperous with its rice plants
great with clusters of seeds,
shaped like horses' manes.
When it is dry,
muṇṭakam bushes grow by the black waters,
its mud dries up,
and the dark backwaters yield white salt.
A fine place, our town, always productive.
Smoke rises from cooking fish and winds through the street,
its meaty smell making the beach pleasant
where *ñāḻal* bushes have tiny flowers.
And yet, friend, there is one fault with our town.
In the grove, bees get drunk
on the pollen of black-stalked *puṉṉai* flowers
and then buzz
so we cannot hear the bells
of his tall chariot.

Ulōccaṉār

[According to the modern commentator Duraicami Pillai, this poem is uttered by the friend to the heroine, who has become despondent at the gossip about her affair with the hero. The friend makes the point that, with all the good things that are happening to the heroine, she should not become despondent at the gossip.]

Naṟṟiṇai 314

When old age comes,
when youth is over,
happiness like that I had with him
is gone forever.
He would hold me close to his chest,
with its garland of moist petals of monsoon jasmine
and its fragrant sandal paste,
and he would press my young warm breasts to him,
flushed with spots and adorned with a sash,
their nipples dark,
and he would say,
"May our nights pass in joy like this."
Yet he has shown himself a liar.
From the swaying top of a *kaḷḷi* tree,
whose unripen fruits seem broken and crushed,
a grey dove cries sadly to his mate
on the long, sun-scorched barrenness
where he has gone.

Muppēr Nākaṉār

Naṟṟiṇai 319

The sound of the ocean is stilled
and the wind, spreading pollen, has dimmed the grove.
On the long wide street of the old, sandy town,
an owl and his mate light on the *ātti* tree at the crossroads
and call out, so people are afraid.
It is midnight,
with its deluding darkness,
a time when demons roam.
I think of my shy little woman
whose round, soft arms are supple as bamboo,
whose beauty many liken to a doll's.
I think of pressing to me
her lovely breasts flushed with spots,
and even when the fish close their eyes and sleep
I do not sleep.

Viḷakkuṭic Cokiraṉār

[A crossroads is an especially dangerous place, since all sorts of people pass by, some of whom may infect it with dangerous powers.]

Naṟṟiṇai 324

Her mother suffers so I do not know
how she will bear it.
Her daughter,
her body like gold,
goes followed by him she loves
in the jungle, where elephants have long tusks.
She runs as if she were playing,
as if she were rolling a ball
in the large house of her beloved father,
whose strong spear has a shaft that glistens as if rubbed with ghee.
Her hair lovely and fine,
she goes on feet as gentle as cotton.

Kayamaṉār

[The heroine is eloping with her lover.]

Naṟṟiṇai 335

The shining moon rises
and the sea,
its dark waters seething on its shores,
does not stop beating.
It surges over low lands, its sound never still.
In the grove with its water and many flowers,
thorny-leafed *tāḻai* opens it tight buds
like curved vessels pouring out cooked rice,
and the wind spreads and carries its unfading fragrance.
The *aṉṟil* bird cries so one's very bones melt
in its anguish at the top of the dark palmyra tree,
and a good lute,
plucked, stroked, coaxed,
is unremitting through the night with its sweet sound.
My desire is great,
there is no one to help it.

Veḷḷi Vītiyār

[The word I have translated "coaxed" means literally "as fingers change strings."]

Naṟṟiṇai 350

In Iruppai city ruled by King Virāaṉ, who gives chariots away,
flocks of birds in the field,
frightened by the kettle drums of men harvesting white paddy,
flee to the bent limbs of a *marutam* tree
and make its flowers drop down.
The beauty I have kept so long is splendid as that city,
yet if it must be spoiled I do not care.
I will not let you close to me,
for if I do,
your hands, seizing and pulling,
can force me to their will.
With sandal rubbed on you from round breasts
and a garland that is withered,
you are like a dirtied ornament.
Do not come to me:
may she who embraces you flourish.

Paraṇar

[The heroine reproaches her husband for going to courtesans.]

Naṟṟiṇai 360

Like girls after a festival
who have danced until the head of the drum is dry,
the women you loved yesterday
have lost all their freshness.
Go now, great one,
enjoy the soft arms of the women they bring you today,
and may your whores flourish.
When you heard what people were saying,
you must have suffered terribly,
like a young bull elephant
that smears the paddy ball in its trunk all over its body
when its driver pricks it with the goad
to make it eat more quickly.
Oh yes, I am happy that you came home,
but remember, you can sleep here anytime.

Ōrampōkiyār

[The heroine scolds her husband.]

Naṟṟiṇai 362

You walked stiff as a puppet
as you left your father's land.
Now, here on the expanse of the meadow
made lovely by the clouds pouring down their cool rain
in the first storm of the season,
see the scarlet beetles,
pick them up,
play with them a bit.
I will go to the sandy place behind the great-trunked *vēṅkai* tree there
whose bark young elephants have rubbed smooth.
If men come to fight me,
I will not be afraid, I will turn them back.
But if your people come,
I will hide, dark one.

Maturai Marutaṉ Iḷanākaṉār

[The hero and heroine have eloped. Here, he says that he will fight with anyone who comes to get her back, except for her relatives, from whom he will hide so that he does not have to fight them.]

Naṟṟiṇai 366

Her loins, ornamented with jewels,
show like a cobra's raised hood
through the fine loose cloth she wears.
She has round arms.
Her hair, dark as blue sapphire, is combed out perfectly
and tied with the fragrant, tiny-stemmed jasmine flowers of the cold
season,
as bees buzz close.
Surely they are the most foolish people on earth
who would leave such a pillow of soft, thick hair
when the wind blows from the north,
touching and opening the white spearlike
buds of sugarcane
and pushing against the nest made by a sparrow
soon to give birth.

Maturai Īḻattup Pūtaṉṟēvaṉār

[The word for foolish—*maṭavar*—is usually used of women. Here it is reversed, as the hero describes the foolishness of men who would leave their women to get wealth. A cobra is conventionally described as having a jewel on its hood.]

Naṟṟiṇai 369

The sun, its rage exhausted, reaches its mountain.
A flock of sparrows, their wings spread wide, passes through the sky.
The day, bit by bit, is spent
and jasmine opens its bud-mouths.
If evening with its emptiness comes today,
I do not know, friend,
how I will bear my desire
as hard to hold back as the flood
that rages uncontrolled beyond the shore of the great Ganges,
fed by a white, glittering waterfall
roaring from the rain-soaked Himalayan heights,
where *ñemai* trees tower high.

Maturai Mēlaik Kaṭaiyattār Nalveḷḷaiyār

Naṟṟiṇai 371

Like golden-flowered *koṉṟai* trees on a green hill,
the clouds flash into the crevices of a dark mountain.
They spread, covering the vast sky
in the land where my dark woman is,
and begin the first rain of the season.
In her pain she grows thin and her glistening bangles are loosened on her arms.
She begins to weep,
she whose ornaments are lovely.
At that, the cowherds begin to play their flutes,
like thunder whose voice quivers in the night.

Auvaiyār

[The hero imagines the state of the woman he left as the monsoon begins.]

Naṟṟiṇai 378

The night is long
and my desire grows so I cannot close my eyes.
The crashing waves of the cool sea
move in measured time
like the beat of a drum,
slowly, like a man limping with an old wound.
Yet whether the waves torment me
or whether they relent,
the night does not pass,
the dawn does not come.
That loose-mouthed women sing of my paleness
is the fruit of my love
for the man who came and knocked down our small sandhouses
with tiny little designs on the towering dunes,
who said kind words that I believed,
he from a shore where water roars and crashes.

Vaṭavaṇṇakkaṉ Pēricāttaṉār

Akanāṉūṟu

Akanāṉūṟu 16

His palms as red
as the petals of a lotus
showing its pollen-covered filaments as it blooms in stagnant water
  where otters live,
his pretty mouth red as coral,
his unclear words delightful,
our gold-bangled son whom anyone would love
was playing in the street with his toy chariot.
When she saw that he was alone,
that woman with her bright teeth approached
and, as no one was looking,
thinking how like his father he was
she took him to her young breasts
adorned with ornaments and heavy with gold
and said happily, "Come, my life."
I saw her standing there.
I did not leave but said,
"Beautiful woman, don't be shy.
You are his mother too."
And quickly I embraced her.
Seeing her then as she stood ashamed,
looking down as if she were a thief
and scratching the ground with her toe,
how, my lord, could I not love her?
who was like the goddess of chastity
full of power in the heavens,
who was like the mother of your son.

Marutam
Cākalācaṉār

[This poem is uttered by the heroine to her husband. The woman described in the poem is the courtesan, whom the husband visits. Even though the courtesan is older than the heroine, she has not had any children, and so her breasts are still young. The goddess of chastity in the sky is the star Arundhatī.]

Akanāṉūṟu 22

With his broad, sweet-smelling chest,
the man from mountains
where massed waterfalls drop from high, demon-infested summits
bewitched me.
The people of my town did not know the cause of my pain.
"If we worship the long-speared god
whose mighty hands are famed
for crushing *all* who do *not* bow *to him*,
she will recover,"
women who know the ancient arts said
as if it were the truth.
They arranged the place of worship,
garlanded the spear,
sang so the town resounded,
offered sacrifice,
spread lovely red millet and blood,
and worshipped Murugan.
On that same fearful midnight,
my lover came fragrant with sandal paste,
wearing flowers swarming with bees
that had blossomed thickly in a remote mountain cave,
eluding the guards of the tall house like a strong tiger
that moves hidden,
its stealthy gaze searching for an elephant to kill.
His heart filled with desire, he did everything I wanted,
and each time he embraced me,
making my sweet life melt,
my whole body filled with laughter
as I thought
that while it was my lover who had come
to cure the pain he had caused,

they would say
the cure was from the useless priest of Murugan.

Kuṟiñci
Veṟipāṭiya Kāmakkaṇṇiyār

Akanāṉūṟu 66

"Those fortunate enough to have children
of unblemished appearance,
loved even by their enemies,
shine in this life with their fame
and come to the other world without sin."
Such is the proverb,
and I found out how true it is, friend.
Wearing a full garland on his chest,
yesterday my man wanted to enjoy one of his women.
With a new ornament, he was going along this street,
bells ringing on his fine horses.
As he passed in front of our door,
our flower-eyed son ran out with his unsure steps
wishing to see him.
"Stop the tall chariot, driver," he said,
and got down.
At once he embraced the child,
holding him so his coral-red mouth pressed his chest.
"Now, charioteer, to her house," he said,
but his son cried, not letting him go.
Looking like the god of wealth himself,
he entered with the boy.
I felt ashamed,
was worried that he would think I had arranged it,
and so I scolded the child,
took up a stick,
and waving it in my hand I said,
"He gets in your way and has not behaved himself."
But he took the child to him,
and even with the pleasant beat of the drum with a trembling head
seemed to call to her house,
he was not tempted.

He remembered how he had been nice to me
the day I and my friends played *kaḻaṅku*,
and in his guilt
he gave up the thought of seeing his women.

Marutam
Cellūrk Kōcikaṉ Kaṇṇaṉār

[*Kaḻaṅku* means "molucca beans." Here it probably refers to a game played with those beans. Presumably, the hero first met his future wife when she was playing the game with her friends.]

Akanāṉūṟu 72

The lightning seems to rip the darkness.
The skies pour down drops in the heavy midnight rain.
A bear with large paws pulls on a termite mound
whose broken front swarms with fireflies,
glimmering like sparks from beaten metal,
and as he digs out its comb
he is like a blacksmith forging iron.
The paths there are difficult.
In the river are terrible crocodiles
that men shiver to think of.
It roars against rocks with its torrent
and breaks the poles of boatmen.
Yet he did not think, "I am afraid, I am alone."
On those demon-haunted slopes that rustle with swaying bamboo,
so high it seems to hold up the clouds,
to satisfy the hunger of his pregnant mate
who nurtures two lives,
an angry tiger kills a boar,
and in the light of a jewel dropped by a cobra
to hunt in its rays
he drags the body along as its blood thickens.
The forking paths there are like swords to walk on,
the rock-strewn ways strike fear into those who even think of them
He who came there, carrying his spear, his heart full of love,
is not a cruel person,
and you who told him to come then
did no wrong.
I filled you with all my worries, friend.
I am to blame.

Kuṟiñci
Erumai Veḷiyaṉār Makaṉār Kaṭalaṉār

[In this poem the heroine addresses her friend, who has arranged for the hero to meet her at night. In Tamil, cobras are thought to carry sapphires on their heads. They put these light-emitting jewels down at night and search for prey with their rays.]

Akanāṉūṟu 77

"Leaving her lovely face to grow pale,
it would be a fine thing
if I were to gather wealth,
adventuring in the difficult wilderness."
This plan took over my heart
without my knowing its danger.
In the burning heat, thunder-spitting clouds have gone away,
people stop and point out old, barren places
deserted by those who lived there,
and like officials who examine seals and break them
before they take palmyra-leaf ballots from rope-bound pots,
red-eared vultures pick up the intestines of men
who gave their lives for victory in battle
and spread them out so one feels dread
on rock-covered, forking roads.
Should I go there,
then in the evening when darkness grows sharp
and the strong wind comes in waves
through the spotted shadows
of the smooth-trunked *itti* tree in the village,
her eyes filling with cool tears will strike me down
like the straight-bladed spear
raised in hard battle against enemy kings
by Piṭṭaṉ, the Chera warrior, always drunk,
his curved bow in his strong hand.

Pālai
Marutaṉ Iḷanākaṉār

Akanāṉūṟu 82

Many saw him
as he stood with a flowering garland on his chest
near the entrance of the field of ripe millet
and asked which way the elephant he was fighting had gone,
carefully choosing an arrow
and holding in his hand his strong, well-shaped bow,
he from a land
where the summer westwind makes flute music
in the shining holes bored by bees in swaying bamboo,
where the pleasant sound of cool waters dropping from a waterfall
is the thick voice of many concert drums,
where the harsh cries of a herd of deer are the brass trumpets,
where the bees on the flowering mountain slopes are the lutes,
and where,
as an audience of monkeys looks on with delight,
a peacock swaying happily
looks like a dancing woman entering the stage.
Friend, of all those who saw him,
why am I the only one who,
lying on my bed in the night with its difficult darkness,
my eyes streaming tears,
feel my arms grow thin?

Kuṟiñci
Kapilar

Akanāṉūṟu 98

On a cold mountain whose high slopes were planted with crops,
intending only kindness,
he told me the sweet things he was thinking.
Now the memory has grown bitter
and the pain unbearable
that would go away
if I could embrace the chest
of him whose mountain is demon-haunted.
But mother does not know that.
She sees the loosening of my glittering bangles,
set close and decorated with long lines,
and, helpless, she asks others.
Women skilled at telling lies as if they were ancient truths
spread rice in a winnowing fan and say,
"It is the power of Murugan, hard to bear."
Mother believes them,
and in a temple so perfect it seems a painting, she prays,
"The beauty praised by many,
faultless as a doll's,
should be as before
for my daughter."
Sweet-sounding instruments play all together
and the floor is prepared.
In a large enclosure decorated with ornaments for the dance,
they dress themselves with *kaṭampu* and white pieces of palmyra leaves;
the pleasant drone hums behind the monotonous beat;
they cry out the great name of the god,
throwing up their hands,
and the priest makes a show on the wide floor
with his frenzied dancing,
moving like a puppet handled by a skillful puppeteer.
Because mother desired this, what will happen, friend?

If, now that the dance has been performed,
driving pained women into possession,
my thin body does not regain its loveliness,
it will be impossible for my secret not to become common gossip.
But if, seeing the suffering my wise lover caused me,
the god with a sweet smell and a long spear should show mercy,
and the man from a forested land should hear
that his woman with dense bangles no longer suffers for him,
it will be even harder for me to live.

Kur̲iñci
Ver̲ipāṭiya Kāmakkaṇṇiyār

Akanāṉūṟu 110

If mother finds out, let her.
And if this lovely little street with its loose mouths hears, let it.
Before the god at Pukār with swift whirlpools,
I swear this is all that happened.
In the grove, I and my garlanded friends played in the sea,
made little houses and heaped up play rice.
Then we were resting a bit,
waiting for our tiredness to go,
when a man came up and said,
"Innocent girls with round, soft arms as supple as bamboo!
The light of the sun has faded and I am very tired.
Would there be anything wrong if I ate a guest's meal
on a soft, open leaf,
and then stayed in your noisy little village?"
Seeing him, we lowered our faces,
and, hiding ourselves, we politely replied,
"This food is not for you.
It is moist fish, eaten only by low people."
Then suddenly someone said,
"There, can't we see the boats coming in
with their tall, waving banners?"
At that we kicked over our sand houses with our feet.
Of all those who were leaving,
he looked straight at me and said,
"O you who have the lovely face, may I go?"
so I felt I had been ruined.
I answered, "You may,"
and he, staring at me all the while,
stood tall, holding the staff of his chariot.
Still it seems to be before my eyes.

Neytal
Pōntaip Pacalaiyār

Akanāṉūṟu 136

They served white rice full of ghee and meat,
perfectly prepared.
Their generosity unbounded, they honored their guests.
As omens fell together favorably, as the sky shone with clear light,
and as the moon came together auspiciously with the wagon constellation,
they readied the marriage house and worshipped the god.
Then the great kettle drum roared with the loud marriage drum;
the girls who had washed her for marriage looked on,
their flowerlike eyes unwinking, and hid themselves;
and her relatives put on her a white thread
and the cool fragrant buds of the tuber *aṟukai*,
whose petals spread dark as polished sapphires
in valleys where large calves
graze on the forked, dull leaves of *vākai* plants
with soft flowers.
And they made her lovely with pure garments.
Then they came, arousing my desire,
and they gave her to me beautiful with ornaments
and wiped off her sweat
in that enclosure where the sound of marriage was like the rain.
That night she, her chastity perfect,
as close to me as my body to my life,
covered herself with her still unwrinkled garment.
I said, "Open it just a little
so the breeze can dry the sweat
from your hot forehead, bright as the crescent moon,"
and, my heart full of desire, I pulled off her garment.
Her form exposed glistened like an unsheathed sword,
and she, unable to hide,
took off the bright garland of lilies that held her braids
and covered herself
with the darkness of her thick black hair
full of flowers humming with bees,
and, ashamed, begged and pleaded with me.

Marutam
Viṟṟūṟṟu Mūteyiṉaṉār

Akanāṉūṟu 158

"At midnight when darkness lay thick
and the rain had stopped
after pouring down from great clouds with thunder and lightning,
when all was still
I saw her,
her heavy earrings flashing like lightning in the sky,
her thick curly hair let loose down her back,
walking carefully
like a peacock coming down a mountain
as she descended from the platform out in the field."
Listen, mother, you shouldn't frighten me by saying these things.
On the haunted slope where our garden is,
a spirit comes wearing bright flowers,
taking whatever form it wishes.
There dreams that seem to be real
deceive the sleeping.
Even if she is alone without a light,
this girl trembles.
And if an owl in the courtyard *marā* tree hoots,
her heart quivers and she looks for a place to hide.
And father, as strong and angry as Murugan, is at home
and has let his dogs, like a pack of tigers, run loose.
She is much too afraid to have done what you say.

Kuṟiñci
Kapilar

[The friend of the heroine speaks to the foster mother.]

Akanāṉūṟu 224

Go, driver! The sun's light is growing dim,
and my woman must be thinking to herself:
"His horses, held back by the reins in the hands of the skillful driver,
breathe hot like a bellows pumped rapidly by a smith.
Their heads under the cruel yoke, their gaits swift,
they go, quick as the wind.
Their mouths drip pure white spittle
like lumps of butter floating in the foam of churned milk
that grows thin as it flows down
and, scattering, light as a spiderweb,
splashes his chest coated with dry sandal paste.
On the meadow that is no longer hot,
lovely to see with its fresh beauty,
a herd of deer leaps and scatters.
The whirling rims of his wheels split the sand
with the musical sound of a food mill
turned by a housewife grinding dry grain.
Will he come back, friend, who is the companion of my life?"
And, pushing tight her bright bangles decorated with a few lines,
she with her perfect ornaments must be pitiful
as she looks again and again
from her large, guarded house.

Mullai
Āvūr Mūlaṅkiḻār Makaṉār Peruntalaic Cāttaṉār

[The hero addresses his charioteer as he returns from war, his thoughts on his reunion with his wife.]

Akanāṉūṟu 261

In her hair lovely with its five braids
she put bright *pātiri* flowers with black outer petals
taken from the spring grove
and she mixed them with *atiral*.
On her body she put *marāam* flowers,
their soft clusters moist with sweet juice.
She swung her arms so her dense, bright bangles jingled
and she walked slowly, a few steps at a time,
and her anklets seemed to tinkle with laughter.
"Go ahead a little
so I can see your lovely back," I said,
but she was ashamed and stood to the side,
her shame showing in her deerlike eyes
as she bowed her head.
Nor would I go first,
and so we stopped in that difficult wilderness
listening to the roaring of a great tiger
after he had killed an elephant
and the wild rhythms of *tuṭi* drums
from forest villages where drunken bowmen
beat them in frenzy.

Pālai
Pālaipāṭiya Peruṅkaṭuṅkō

Akanāṉūṟu 276

In a long, dark pond
a silvery scabbard fish sets out to hunt prey.
Suddenly he sees the foot of a heron
that would eat him
and very slowly,
quivering like a thief who has entered a house and found guards,
he pulls back.
That is what happened in my man's town.
Come what may,
I feel no more shame from being with him.
No, let all our street see us,
and let his women, their red-lined eyes blackened with collyrium, look on.
I'll hold his garland and his garment
and, as if he were a great bull elephant
lured by a female whom the Aryans have trained,
I'll use his arm as a post,
tie my hair to him,
and watch over him.
Should I fail to do this,
then like the wealth of a rich man
who will give nothing to suppliants in need,
may the beauty my mother nourished spoil,
hoarded only for myself.

Marutam
Paraṇar

Akanāṉūṟu 280

Like gold piled up,
many flowers of bright-clustered *cerunti*
covered her hair
as she played, kicking at the crabs
on the shore heaped high with thick sand,
and then rested.
I know that even if I gave many jewels and great wealth,
I could not have that girl whose bangles are lovely.
But if I were to come here to live
so that her father could know me,
if I were to harvest the salt on the shore of the great waters with him,
ride out on a raft with him to the deep sea,
obey him, follow him, be with him,
then perhaps he would be fair
and give her to me,
that fisherman from a harbor with a lovely grove,
where they take fat pearls from the spreading waves
and divide them on the broad shore humming with dragonflies.

Neytal
Ammūvaṉār

Akanāṉūṟu 298

In your land,
when in the evening dark as blue sapphire
the *vēṅkai* tree fills with yellow blossoms,
it is like the sun rising with many rays from the brimming sea,
bountiful,
ascending and shining to light the day's work.
The wind swirls laden with cool drops
and caresses its flourishing branches
glistening with bright shoots.
At midnight you came,
waving off the bees
that swarmed around your low-hanging garland
with its soft opening clusters,
carrying a spear so white it seemed to cut the hard darkness,
making your way along a forest path
on that prosperous mountain
where a great elephant moves proudly with ichor streaming down his temples,
still caught by a rage for killing
and not calm enough yet to rejoin his mates.
That is how my lover came,
but it was even sweeter for me to see
how willing my friend was to comfort me:
I was in the large guarded house of my father,
whose chariot is swift, whose drink is like the rain.
Mother was watching me,
and I was afraid she would know.
So in the middle of the night,
restraining my feelings,
I did not speak of my desire
but talked of your cruelty.
My friend knew my real feelings and she said,
"Don't be sad.
He who left you will come;

he will not delay,"
and through the whole sleepless night
she stayed with me.

Kuṟiñci
Maturaip Paṇṭavāṇikaṉ Iḷantēvaṉār

[The heroine, unable to go out and meet her lover at night because she is guarded by her mother, is consoled by her friend.]

Akanāṉūṟu 308

In your land, sheets of rain and hail beat down in the night,
washing the deep wound that has slowed an elephant's walk
after fighting a tiger.
Then, at the dawn,
a pure white waterfall roars down with a flood of water
and the white clouds surrounding and covering the glistening mountain
are like the smoke of a potter's kiln.
Why should you come at night?
If you come in the day,
you can pass your time with me,
chasing parrots from the tiny-grained millet
as we stand on the platform
raised by my hot-tempered father, whose spear never misses,
near the stone cave too high for elephants to reach.
And you can sleep with my soft hair for your pillow,
full of many fragrant, bright, pollen-filled waterlily flowers
taken from the spring that gushes on the green slope.
You can pass your time like that,
and then,
like a great elephant
that has groped its way through a field
carefully guarded by watchmen,
you can return to the town of black-stalked *kuṟiñci*
where you live your pleasant life.

Kuṟiñci
Picirāntaiyār

Akanāṉūṟu 316

In his town,
an old buffalo, his back wet and cool, his horns curved,
grazes on bright-flowered lilies
in a pond full of water and fish,
sleeps all night in the oozing mud,
and then when dawn comes
walks out, crushing murrel fish with their fresh-smelling fat,
drapes himself with bright *pakaṉṟai* creepers,
and enters the ancient town like a warrior victorious in battle.
Tell me, woman of the house,
why are you angry with your man?
Why do you say,
"He brings women in his chariot, their ornaments exquisite,
their arms thin with desire for him,
so many the city cannot hold them all,
and they offer themselves to him again and again.
How can he bear living such a life?"
Surely a wife is foolish to show
such anger even though she knows
that women strong enough to quarrel and live apart
must do without the goddess of prosperity,
must sift the stones from a small portion of rice,
cook it, and eat alone,
must suffer their sweet-voiced children
to suck their dried-up breasts.

Marutam
Ōrampōkiyār

[The buffalo is compared to a fighting man, who returns covered with gore from battle and decked with the garlands of victory. The comparison is ironic, for the buffalo is meant to be likened to the hero. In the words of the modern commentary, "By saying that in his town, a buffalo grazes on lilies in the tank, sleeps in the mud, and then at dawn destroys murrel fish, drapes himself with *pakaṉṟai*, and enters the ancient town like a warrior, [the poet means] that the hero enjoys the harlots in that quarter [of town], spends the entire night in that base pleasure, and in the morning leaves, making his reputation small and causing much gossip."]

Akanāṉūṟu 339

Yoked to swift horses the tall chariot speeds.
Into the tracks left by its strong-spoked wheels
water runs swiftly
like a darting snake.
Unripened on the stalk
beans decay like loosening fists.
The cold season has come.
In my heart, I resolve to set out,
to do a man's work.
My boldness urges me on,
my desire pulls me back,
I do not know what to do.
Unable to decide,
I am like an ant caught inside a bamboo torch
with flames burning at both ends.
Surely she would grieve, she who is so delicate.
For her, love is like the bond between life and body,
passion is like life itself.
For her, separation would be like death.

Pālai
Naraimuṭineṭṭaiyār

Akanāṉūṟu 374

Drinking from the great ocean,
darkening the directions,
powerfully rising and spreading over the broad earth,
the clouds, heavy with rain,
flash all together with lightning as if they were splitting the sky,
descend in a great mass,
pour down shower upon shower as if overturned,
and with the roaring of their thunder
rain down breaking drops whose sweet sounds
are like music from the strings of lutes plucked by bards.
Then after the downpour they leave,
and in the flower-fragrant dawn,
on the road where salty soil appears among the thick heaped sand,
small-bellied red beetles run in tiny steps
and disappear in lovely faded *kāyā* flowers,
like coral mixing with blue sapphires.
Now, at this time of desire,
when the beauty of the rains is everywhere,
drive the chariot with all your skill
and let the woman with perfect ornaments, a tiny waist, and round arms
welcome her husband back.

Mullai
Iṭaikkāṭaṉār

[The hero, returning home from war, addresses his charioteer.]

Akanāṉūṟu 375

"He will not stay away for long,
and yet you do not stop your worrying,"
you say, friend.
In the hot, frightening wilderness he has entered,
wild young warriors whose shouts echo on forking paths
test their arrow shots,
killing travellers, even though they have no money,
and feed them to the birds.
There, while foxes move around them,
vultures eat fat,
their strong, close-set claws bloody
as they sit on a large-trunked *yā* tree,
on a branch as thick as the trunk of the elephant
that killed the northern newcomers,
crushing their soft heads,
when Iḷamperuñceṉṉi, the Chola king,
whose thick arms always gain victory in battle,
sure in his shining fame,
crushed the fortress of Pāḻi with its coppery walls
to finish the work of his line.
Even though I know he will return safely,
my eyes, friend, refuse to stop crying.

Pālai
Iṭaiyaṉ Cēntaṉ Koṟṟaṉār

Akanāṉūṟu 390

They shout out the price of salt harvested from salt flats;
they travel to far distances on dusty roads
as they go in their caravans over long trails
carrying thick staffs.
The life of these salt merchants seems a good one to me.
Her curly hair tossing,
the dress of shoots she wears to ornament her wide, soft loins
swaying with each step,
she cries in every street,
"People of the town! Salt is as cheap as paddy!
Will you buy some?"
"Listen, you with your belly curved and arms supple as bamboo,
you did not tell us the price of the salt of your body,"
I said, standing a little away.
Her anger showing in her large, red-lined eyes blackened with collyrium,
she said, "You, over there, who are you?"
And innocent,
very lovely,
she moved off a little,
smiling,
her few rows of white bangles flashing,
taking my heart with her.

Neytal
Ammūvaṉār

Puṟanāṉūṟu

Puṟanāṉūṟu 19

Surrounded by the roaring seas,
this dense earth has a place, Talaiyālaṅkāṉam,
where Tamils clashed.
There you showed that lives are many,
Death is one,
Ceḻiyaṉ of the conquering spear.
"Your chest is like a great rock door
set carefully in a trap by a tiger hunter,"
I thought anxiously, and so I embraced you
with your polished, glittering necklace of pearls.
Now on that field, women of ancient houses
weep with melting hearts and they say,
"Like a flock of little birds resting together on a hill,
arrows have pierced the mortally wounded elephant.
Cut off, its strong hollow trunk and mouth
roll on the ground like a plow.
That is how with raised swords they won the battle.
Now our sons, the hair still sparse on their faces,
lie dead with our husbands
and we have a victory."
Death himself is ashamed and feels pity
on that dreadful field
where you conquered the strength of the seven.

Kuṭapulaviyaṉār sings Pāṇṭiyaṉ Neṭuñceḻiyaṉ.

[See Puṟanāṉūṟu 276-279 for other poems describing the reaction of mothers to their sons' death in battle. The poem is integrated in a way that I find impossible to reproduce in English. Literally, it reads, " . . . and so I embraced, did I not, O you who conquered as women wept saying . . . , your breast."]

Puṟanāṉūṟu 20

One might measure the depth of the dark sea,
the width of the earth,
the regions of the winds,
the empty, eternal sky,
but he could never measure you,
your wisdom, kindness, compassion.
Those who live in your shade
know no other flames than the blazing of the red sun
and the fire that cooks their rice.
They know no warrior's bow, only the rainbow.
They know no weapon, only the plow.
O lord who devour the lands of others,
destroying your foes with warriors who are skilled in the art of war,
no enemies eat the soil of your land,
only women compelled by the longings of pregnancy.
Arrows are stored in your guarded fortress,
justice lives in your scepter.
Even if new birds come or old birds go,
nothing threatens the benevolence of your rule.
That is why all breathing creatures in your kingdom
live in fear that you might come to harm.

Kuṟuṅkōḻiyūrkiḻār sings Cēramāṉ Yāṉaikkaṭcēy Māntarañcēralirumpoṟai.

[Pregnant women in South India are supposed to eat mud. The new birds are birds of ill omen; the old ones, birds of good omen.]

Puṟanāṉūṟu 21

O lord whose fame is past the skill of poets!
There was a fortress named Kāṉappēr.
Its moat was deeper than the earth;
its walls seemed to touch the sky;
its bastions were like flowering stars;
the forest that guarded it was so thick with trees
that not a ray entered.
Strong camps surrounded it.
Yet that fortress is gone
like water vaporized by iron
heated in a glowing fire by a black-handed smith,
and Vēṅkaimārpaṉ grieves.
O king wearing the *tumpai* garland of victory every day,
your fame exhausts the conventions of poets.
As they who scorn you perish along with their name,
may your spear flourish, resplendent in its renown.

Aiyūr Mūlaṅkiḻār sings Kāṉappēreyil Kaṭanta Ukkirapperuvaḻuti.

[The name of this king means "The great and terrible Vaḻuti [a title of the Pandyan kings] who vanquished Kāṉappēreyil, the great forest wall." *Tumpai* leaves were worn by victorious kings. The word translated "vaporized" literally means "eaten."]

Puṟanāṉūṟu 25

Driving the darkness away from the star-glittering sky,
unwavering as it rises,
the fearful sun with its intense heat
and the moon shining with mellow light—
both seemed to have been brought to earth
when on the fearful field you killed
the hard-to-conquer kings who had sworn an oath,
and when you seized their tightly laced royal drums.
But then you stopped,
you did not attack with your spear
wielding it until it shattered,
for you saw bright-faced women weeping,
lost in the grief of new widowhood,
striking their breasts until they burned,
and cutting off their thick dark hair
soft and lovely as glistening black sand.

Kallāṭaṉār sings Pāṇṭiyaṉ Talaiyālaṅkāṉattuc Ceruveṉṟa Neṭuñceḻiyaṉ.

[In ancient Tamilnad, widows had to shave their heads and practice severe asceticism, if they did not take their own lives in suttee. The king addressed in this poem sees the austerities that the widows of his dead enemies must undergo and is moved to abandon battle.]

Puṟanāṉūṟu 38

Victorious king on a young mountainous elephant,
whose great army has waving flags of many colors
that seem to wipe the sky!
Where you glance angrily, fire spreads;
where you look with favor, gold blossoms.
If you wish the sun to shed moonlight
or the moon to burn with the heat of the sun,
your wish comes true.
What worth can I have who have been born and raised in your shadow?
Even they who live in sweet paradise,
with groves of golden flowers,
though they receive reward for the good they have done,
do not enjoy perfect happiness,
for there are no rich there to give and no poor to ask.
But since the pleasures of that place are found here also,
even in the countries of your enemies,
suppliants think of your land
because you live in it.

The song of Āvūr Mūlaṅkiḻār to Cōḻaṉ Kuḷamuṟṟattut Tuñciya Kiḷḷivaḷavaṉ, in reply to that king's question, "Did you think of me? What is your country?"

Puṟanāṉūṟu 42

O lord of unending generosity and fierce battle,
your elephant is like a mountain,
your army roars like the sea,
your spear flashes like lightning.
You have the might, great one,
to make the heads of the earth bow low,
and so there is no lack in your land.
Nor is this new.
In your country, people hear only the sound of cool water,
never, even in dreams, the sound of your advancing army
making them cry out, "Stay away, lord Vaḷavaṉ!"
Your land is guarded like a cub watched over by a tiger:
your scepter never grows thin.
Your good country has the prosperity of great victories.
In it are towns set in fertile lands
where men give in hospitality to relatives from dry lands
vālai fish taken by harvesters from the lowest sluices
and tortoises turned over by the plows of farmers
and sugar from cane cut by workmen
and waterlilies picked by girls bringing water from the great tanks.
Like many rivers that rush from mountains
toward the great sea
and descend into it from the edge of the land,
all poets come towards you.
And you, strong and angry as Death
when he swings his mace and brings incurable pain,
you go towards the lands of the two kings who are your enemies.

Kōvūrkiḻār sings Cōḻaṉ Kuḷamuṟṟattut Tuñciya Kiḷḷivaḷavaṉ.

Puṟanāṉūṟu 43

Astounding even the sages with long matted hair
who, to relieve the suffering of those who live in this world,
eat only wind as they circle around with the sun
and bear the heat of its fierce rays,
your great forefather, unstinting in his generosity,
placed himself on the scale,
afraid that the dove of tiny steps that had taken refuge with him
might be harmed by the sharp-clawed, bent-winged vulture.
Younger brother of Tērvaṇkiḷḷi,
who has wealth and the valor to conquer enemies,
lord of Maṟavaṉs with curved bows and long arrows!
Generous chief with swift horses,
I was angry and said to you sarcastically,
"I have my doubts about you.
Your ancestors who wore garlands of *ār* never hurt Brahmins.
How is it that you are not like them?"
At that you were ashamed, as if you had done something wrong,
even though I was really at fault.
You showed then that men of your line
easily tolerate the offenses of others.
O you who are handsome with your strength,
it is I who am wrong.
May your life be good
and last more days
than there are grains of sand
piled into dunes by the Kāviri
with its sweet abundant flow.

As Tāmappalkaṇṇaṉār was playing *vaṭṭu* with Māvaḷattāṉ, the younger brother of Cōḻaṉ Nalaṅkiḷḷi, he said to [Māvaḷattāṉ], who, angry because he had hidden a piece, threw a *vaṭṭu* at him, "You are not the son of the Chola king." Thereupon Māvaḷattāṉ was ashamed. This is Tāmappalkaṇṇaṉār's song to him.

[The beginning of the poem describes ascetics who fast, sitting beneath the sun. Exactly what is meant by "circle around with the sun" is unclear. If Gopalakrishnamacaryar, a modern subcommentator on the *Tirukkuṟaḷ*, is to be believed, the game which occasioned this poem is similar to the modern game of *kōḻi*. Certainly, it was played on a specially marked space, as Tirukkuṟaḷ 401 says, "Like playing *vaṭṭu* without a marked space is making expositions without [the knowledge] of many books." *Kōḻi* has many variants, all of which involve standing behind a line and throwing small balls, which one uses to knock aside other balls or which one tries to get into holes. In at least one variant of the game, the winner of a throw collects balls from his other opponents, the ultimate winner being determined partly by who has amassed the most balls by the end of the game. It is this variant which is evidently being played by the king and the poet in this poem. The forefather of Māvaḷattāṉ is supposed to have been Cempiyaṉ, a Tamilization of the Sanskrit name Śibi. That king is supposed to have given refuge to a dove fleeing from a hawk. In order to save the dove, the king offered the hawk the dove's weight of his own flesh. He placed the dove on one side of a scale and began to cut off his own flesh and to place it on the other side. However much flesh he put, it did not equal the dove's weight, so finally he climbed onto the scale. At that, the dove and hawk assumed their real forms, Dharma and the god Indra, and praised the generosity of the king.]

Puṟanāṉūṟu 47

We hope for patrons,
travel like birds,
and cross wastelands as if they were short,
singing as well as we can with our stumbling tongues.
We find happiness in what we get,
feed our families,
eat without saving,
give without stinting,
and suffer for reputation.
Does this life of a suppliant ever bring harm to others?
Only if you count how we put our enemies to shame in every contest,
walking with our heads held high in joy.
Our lives are no worse than yours
with your fame and the wealth you have gained from ruling the earth.

Kōvūrkiḻār sang this song when Kāriyāṟṟut Tuñciya Neṭuṅkiḷḷi was about to kill a poet named Iḷantattaṉ, thinking him a spy, when he came into Uṟaiyūr from Cōḻaṉ Nalaṅkiḷḷi, and saved him.

Puṟanāṉūṟu 50

Its black sides glisten,
long straps fastened to them faultlessly.
It shines with a garland
woven of long, full peacock feathers,
blue-sapphire dark,
with bright spots,
and is splendid with golden shoots of *uḻiñai*.
Such is the royal drum, hungry for blood.
Before they brought it back from its bath
without knowing I climbed on to its bed
and lay on the covering of soft flowers
that was like a froth of oil poured down.
Yet you were not angry,
you did not use your sharp sword.
Surely that was enough for all of the Tamil lands to learn of it.
But you did not stop there.
You came up to me,
you raised your strong arm, as big around as a concert drum;
you fanned me
and made me cool.
Mighty lord, you must have done these things
because you know that except for those
whose fame is spread across the broad earth
no one has a place for long in the high world of paradise.

Mōcikīraṉār sings Cēramāṉ Takaṭūreṟinta Peruñcēralirumpoṟai, who, when Mōcikīraṉār climbed on the bed of the royal drum which had been taken out to be given a bath in ignorance, did not commit the mistake [of executing him], but took up a chowry and fanned him until he awoke.

[The royal drum, or *muracu*, which is the subject of this poem, was made from a special tree, the tutelary tree of an enemy king, and from special skin. It was beaten in the morning to awaken the king, during battle, and on other important occasions. By being beaten, its sacred power was invoked, for a god was actually thought to reside inside the drum. That is why any desecration of the royal drum, or even of its table, was treated as a serious offense: by such desecration, the very sacred power of the king was threatened.]

Puṟanāṉūṟu 51

No shelter can save you from a flood of water;
no shadow can shade you from intense fire;
nothing can stand against a great wind.
When he is angry and brightly shining,
no one conquers Vaḻuti in battle.
If men say, "Rulers share the cool land of the Tamils,"
he cannot bear it,
but takes up arms and asks for tribute.
Then those kings who say, "Take what you want!"
do not have to tremble.
But pitiful, pitiful, are those who do not earn his grace.
Like winged drones swarming from the red mounds
built with great labor by hoards of tiny termites,
they barely live out the day.

Aiyūr Muṭavaṉār sings Pāṇṭiyaṉ Kūṭakārattut Tuñciya Māṟaṉ Vaḻuti.

Puṟanāṉūṟu 52

On a high summit haunted by demons
a tiger grows tired of his cave,
stretches, gets up,
and goes wherever he wants,
his hunger for meat urging him after prey,
like you when you went off to kill
and the northern kings withered before you,
Vaḻuti of the well-made chariot,
cruel and angry in the fight.
Because you have committed yourself to battle,
the rulers of this great earth are to be pitied.
In their countries,
every town had long banners of smoke
fragrant with the smell of cooking fish
that would wind around the bent branches
of the *marutam* trees in the paddy fields.
Now those lands have lost their wealth
and turned to wastelands.
Their public places are desolate.
Gods who were once loudly worshipped have left their columns,
no longer receiving sacrifices,
and speckled forest hens have filled with eggs
the well-built gambling houses
whose floors have been pitted by game pieces
set down by white-haired old men.

Marutaṉ Iḷanākaṉār sings Pāṇṭiyaṉ Kūṭakārattut Tuñciya Māṟaṉ Vaḻuti.]

Puṟanāṉūṟu 65

The drums are no longer smeared with mud.
The lutes play no more *rāgas*.
The large pots have been overturned and cannot hold ghee.
No longer do his comrades drink liquor so sweet
that bees swarm around it.
The plowmen are silent,
and on the wide streets of the villages no festivals pass.
On the great day of the full moon,
sun and moon face each other
and one of them vanishes behind its mountain
in the dullness of the evening.
Just so, a king like him
aimed at his chest and threw his spear
but wounded his back.
Ashamed, that brave king faced north with his sword,
and here,
the day with its sunlight
is not the same as the days we once knew.

The song of Kaḻāttalaiyār on Cēramāṉ Peruñcēralātaṉ, who did battle with Cōḻaṉ Karikāṟ Peruvaḷattāṉ and, ashamed of the back wound he received in battle, faced north, to commit ritual suicide by fasting to death.

[Presumably, the enemy king saw Peruñcēralātaṉ standing with his back to him, thought he was facing him (a mistake natural enough in the heat of battle), and threw his spear at him. Thus Peruñcēralātaṉ received a wound in his back, something that was cause for great shame among the Tamils, as among other ancient martial peoples, for it implied that the wounded man ran from battle. The king, disgraced, decided to commit suicide in the rite called *vaṭakkiruttal*, in which he faced north, with his sword and shield by his side, and starved himself to death, along with those of his followers who would join him (see the notes on Puṟanāṉūṟu 213 and poems 213-223). The skins of concert drums were polished with mud before they were played. Here, the poet suggests that, in the period of mourning after the king's death, such drums were not played. The sun is used to good effect: by comparing the dying king to the setting sun, the poet suggests that the sun will not rise again; this leads to the final lines of the poem.]

Puṟanāṉūṟu 74

A child born dead,
a child born nothing but a mass of flesh—
my ancestors still thought it was human
and never failed to cut it with the sword.
Has a man sprung from them on this earth
to sit
and suffer like a dog,
in chains,
to beg for the grace of a drink of water from his enemies
to calm the fire in his stomach
that he can no longer bear?

The song of Cēramāṉ Kaṇaikkālirumpoṟai, who fought with Cōḻaṉ Ceṅkaṇāṉ at Tiruppōrppuṟam, was taken prisoner, held in captivity at Kuṭavāyil fortress, and said, "Give me some water," but did not receive it until some time had passed, and, keeping it in his hand and saying that he would not drink, died.

[It was the custom of the ancient Tamils to cut up the bodies of men who died of sickness, so that they would have the good name of having died by the sword and so that their souls could enter into the warriors' afterworld.]

Puṟanāṉūṟu 77

On his legs he wears warrior's rings
where until today he wore the *kiṇkiṇi* anklets of a child.
On his head, from which the child's tuft has just been cut,
he wears the bright shoots of margosa
and long creepers of *uḻiñai*.
In his hands that have just lost their small bracelets,
he holds a bow
as he stands splendidly at the pole of his high chariot.
Who is he?
Let us praise the flowers in his hair!
Though he wears a garland,
he has not taken off the *tāli* of a child.
Only today is he weaned from milk to solid food!
He shows no pride, no scorn to the warriors coming at him angrily,
one after another.
Nor does it make him happy or boastful
that as the sound rises in the broad sky
he takes hold of them,
overturns them,
brings them to the earth,
and kills them.

Iṭaikkuṉṟūrkiḻār sings Pāṇṭiyaṉ Talaiyālaṅkāṉattuc Ceruveṉṟa Neṭuñceḻiyaṉ.

[Margosa was used for garlands by Pandyan royalty. *Uḻiñai* was often worn in battle. At some point in childhood, perhaps when a boy was weaned as in this poem (an event that probably did not take place until the child was about six), the little ringing anklets called *kiṇkiṇi* and the protective amulet worn around the neck called a *tāli* were taken off, and the tuft of hair was cut.]

Puranāṉūṟu 78

His legs strong and lithe,
his bravery fierce and unyielding,
my lord is like a tiger living in a cramped cave
who stretches, rises up, and sets out for his prey.
But they did not think him hard to fight against.
They rose up bellowing,
"We are best, we are the greatest.
Our enemy is young and there is much plunder."
Those foolish warriors who came with contempt
ran with dim eyes, showing their backs,
but he did not let them be killed then.
He took them to the city of their fathers,
and as their women with fine ornaments died in shame
and the clear *kiṇai* drum sounded,
there he killed them.

Iṭaikkuṉṟūrkiḻār sings Pāṇṭiyaṉ Talaiyālaṅkāṉattuc Ceruveṉṟa Neṭuñceḻiyaṉ.

[Like the preceding poem, this concerns the youthful valor of Neṭuñceḻiyaṉ. The description of the wives of the defeated enemies is ironic: they will soon be widows and will no longer wear their ornaments. The *kiṇai* drum was played by the pariah, who even today is the drummer at funerals.]

Puṟanāṉūṟu 82

A festival at hand,
his wife in labor,
the sun setting through pouring rain:
the needle flashes in the hand of the low-born man
as he makes a leather cot.
Swift as that
was the fighting of the lord with a chaplet of *ār*
against the warrior come to take his city.

Cāttantaiyār sings Pōrvaikkōperunaṟkiḷḷi.

[According to the modern commentator Duraisami Pillai, this poem concerns the wrestling contest of Perunaṟkiḷḷi with Mūkkavaṉāṭṭu Amūr Mallaṉ, the subject of poem 80. If so, the translation needs to be emended to read, "as swift as that was the wrestling of the lord . . . with the fighter come to take [the title in] his city." This translation, however, seems unsatisfactory, for poem 81, obviously not about a wrestling match, intervenes. Rather, I would say that this poem describes the same battle as Puṟanāṉūṟu 81, which it matches quite well. This interpretation is also supported by the remarks of Pērāciriyar translated below. The low one—that is, one of low caste—can no longer stitch, once the sun has set. Nor can he seek the help of friends, for it is raining outdoors. But his wife must have a bed to lie on to deliver her child: even today, a bed is a ritual necessity for childbirth. Moreover, the low one is obliged to assist at the festival, which will presumably begin after the sun has set. Mention of the social status of the man stitching the cot implies that stitching is his caste occupation, and that he is extremely skilled in that work, just as the king is skilled in fighting. The remarks of Pērāciriyar in his commentary on the *Tolkāppiyam* (*Uvamaiyiyal*, *Cūttiram* 20) are perceptive: "[The poet] qualifies the figure, needle, with many attributes [*viz.*, the wife in labor, the festival, the setting sun, the rain], but he leaves the object of the comparison, the fight, attributing nothing to it. Nonetheless, he intends that the attributes of the figure apply also to the object of comparison. In what way? Because [applying the attributes of the figure to the object] leads [the reader] to conclude that the business of war accelerates, as many kings are vanquished together in a moment by [the hero], who has in mind [the necessity] of preventing [their taking his city] etc., and who looks forward with confidence to the victory celebration and distributing of gifts [which will take place after the battle]." In other words, just as when the low-caste man finishes stitching his bed, the auspicious events of birth and the festival will take place, so when the hero has finished fighting, the auspicious celebration and giving of gifts will transpire.]

Puṟanāṉūṟu 86

You stand and hold the post of my small house,
and you ask, "Where is your son?"
Wherever my son is, I do not know.
This is the womb that carried him,
like a stone cave
lived in by a tiger and now abandoned.
It is on the battlefield that you will find him.

The song of Kāvaṟ Peṇṭu.

[The contrast of the house, whose artificial nature is emphasized by mention of the supporting pillar, with the natural cave of rock is well made. The poet seems to be contrasting the appearance—which is that the son comes from a domestic environment, where everything is constructed for human comfort—with the reality—which is that the son is not at all effeminate or domesticated, that he is actually like the tiger that lives in a natural cave. Another element of the contrast is that the house, with its support, can easily be, unlike the stone cave, destroyed by nature. Another pattern of suggestion is initiated by the implied comparison between the son and the pillar of the house.]

Puṟanāṉūṟu 87

Enemies, be careful when you take the field.
Among us is a warrior
who will face you in battle.
He is like a wheel made over a month
painstakingly
by a carpenter who makes eight chariots
in a day.

Auvaiyār sings Atiyamāṉ Neṭumāṉ Añci.

Pur̲anāṉūr̲u 89

"O dancer whose mounded loins glisten with a string of jewels,
who are innocent,
whose eyes are blackened with collyrium,
whose face shines,
in your large land does anyone know how to fight?"
Listen, king who cannot stop asking questions,
king with a battling army.
In my land live young, strong warriors
who are like snakes that are not afraid
even when you hit them with sticks,
and in my land lives my lord
who hears the clear sound of the wind
resonating against the head of the tight
taṇṇumai drum hanging in the courtyard
and cries out, "It is war!"

Auvaiyār sings Atiyamāṉ Neṭumāṉ Añci.

[Auvaiyār has placed her poem in the mouth of a dancing woman. The *taṇṇumai* drum summoned men to battle.]

Puṟanāṉūṟu 92

You cannot compare them with a lute.
The tenses are wrong, the meanings unclear,
and yet the words of a little son
fill a father with love.
The words of my mouth are like that also,
O Neṭumāṉ Añci
who have taken many enemy forts with guarded walls,
for they make you show your love.

Auvaiyār sings Atiyamāṉ Neṭumāṉ Añci.

Puṟanāṉūṟu 107

Again and again they call out his name:
"Pāri! Pāri!"
Thus do poets with skilled tongues all praise one man.
Yet Pāri is not alone:
there is also the rain to nourish this earth.

Kapilar sings Vēḷ Pāri.

[Poems 105-120 are by Kapilar, one of the greatest Tamil poets (though poem 112 is attributed to Pāri's daughters). They concern Kapilar's patron, Pāri, a chieftain who controlled the mountain of Paṟampu and a small kingdom of about 300 villages. He was renowned for his generosity, which was and is the most important of virtues in South India. Whether out of jealousy or for some other reason, the three great kings—the Chera, Chola, and Pandya—laid siege to Paṟampu. Finally, unable to take the mountain in battle, they gained their end by treachery and had Pāri put to death. Kapilar took Pāri's daughters and attempted to marry them off; however, he could not persuade any kings to marry them, and finally had them married to Brahmins, an end that he was able to accomplish because he himself was a Brahmin. In this poem, the generosity of Pāri is compared to the rains, which feed the earth with no thought of recompense.]

Puṟanāṉūṟu 109

You may think Pāri's mountain
is easy to conquer.
Even though the three of you
with your gigantic royal drums
lay siege to it,
it still has four foods that no farmer needs to grow.
First, the paddylike seed of small-leafed bamboo thrives there.
Second, the fruit of the sweet-pulped jack tree ripens.
Third, the tuber of the rich *vaḷḷi* creeper grows underground.
And, fourth, honey flows on its tall summits,
its color dark and rich as the hives are opened.
Like the sky is his mountain.
Like the stars in the sky are its springs.
Even though your elephants are tied to every tree,
your chariots spread through every field,
you will not take it by fighting.
He will not surrender it by the sword.
But here: I know how you can win it.
If you play little lutes, their strings of rubbed twine,
have your dancing women come behind with thick, fragrant hair,
and go to him dancing and singing,
he will give you his mountain
and his whole land.

Kapilar sings Vēḷ Pāri.

[See the notes on Puṟanāṉūṟu 107.]

Puṟanāṉūṟu 112

That day in the white
light of the moon,
we had our father
and enemies had not taken our mountain.
This day in the white
light of the moon,
kings
whose royal drums beat victory
have taken our mountain
and we have lost
our father.

The song of Pāri's daughters.

[See the notes on Puṟanāṉūṟu 107.]

Puṟanāṉūṟu 113

They would open pots of liquor,
slaughter rams,
cook rice and fine meat
and give them to whoever wanted them—
so rich you were,
such friendship you showed before.
Now Pāri is dead,
I am bewildered and lost.
My eyes stream tears.
I bow and go, praising you,
great-named Paṟampu mountain,
to find men
fit to touch the fragrant dark hair of his daughters,
their wrists decorated with many small bangles.

The song of Kapilar, as he took leave of Paṟampu [mountain] to give in marriage to Brahmins the daughters of Vēḷ Pāri.

[See the notes on Puṟanāṉūṟu 107.]

Puṟanāṉūṟu 114

From here,
and even from there,
you can still see the mountain
of the great king who would give away chariots,
the mountain where,
like paddy balls chewed and spat out by elephants,
liquid oozing from the mash pressed for liquor
muddies his courtyard.

Kapilar said this as he stood and gazed at Paṟampu while he was taking Vēḷ Pāri's daughters [to find someone to marry them].

[See the notes on Puṟanāṉūṟu 107. At first glance, the point of the description of the mountain appears to be the conventional one of enhancing the fertility of the land described. As one thinks about it, however, it becomes apparent that the elephants are meant to be compared to the kings who took Pāri's kingdom, even though they had no need of it, and destroyed it.]

Puṟanāṉūṟu 116

Lilies that bloomed in deep, sweet-water springs
sway open-flowered over their loins,
their eyes are cool and lovely,
their laughter sweet:
the girls walk along forking, grass-choked paths,
through a fence of thorns,
to a courtyard piled with raw cotton,
past a little house,
and there, where gourds have sprouted and *curai* weeds have taken root,
they climb a heap of *īttu* leaves
and count the wagons of merchants loaded with salt.
How the sight hurts me—may my life waste away!
These same girls, before,
would climb to the top of that great mountain
that is like a plateau, always fertile,
where peacocks rise and dance in groves thick with flowers,
and where on the cultivated slopes monkeys jump and play,
and where the trees have so many fruits even out of season
that the monkeys cannot take them all.
And they would count the proud horses and iron weapons
of the kings who had come to fight their father,
kings with conquering armies
who did not know that Pāri,
with his abundant drink and sharp spear in battle,
could not be overcome.

Kapilar sings Vēḷ Pāri.

[See the notes on Puṟanāṉūṟu 107.]

Puranāṉūṟu 117

Even if Saturn darkened,
even if a comet appeared,
even if Venus went south,
the fields were full,
the bushes blossomed with flowers,
and wild cows with big eyes calved near houses
and grazed in long rows on the good grass.
There many fine men lived
because the king's rule was just,
and rains never failed on mountain fields.
Such was the land where green-leafed jasmine opens
like the thorny teeth of a wildcat's kitten,
the land ruled by him
whose daughters have lovely bangles.

Kapilar sings Vēḷ Pāri.

[See the notes on Puṟanāṉūṟu 107. The astronomical phenomena described at the beginning of this poem are all bad omens that presage drought.]

Puṟanāṉūṟu 123

Anyone, if he drinks toddy in the morning
and gets happily drunk by the time he holds court,
can give away chariots.
But Malaiyaṉ, whose good fame never lessens,
gives without getting drunk more tall ornamented chariots
than there are drops in the clouds
that form over rich Mullūr mountain.

Kapilar sings Malaiyamāṉ Tirumuṭikkāri.

[It is common to compare a king's generosity to that of a cloud.]

Puṟanāṉūṟu 159

"My days and years of living are many,
my life does not end."
My mother complains again and again.
With a stick for a leg,
she hobbles with many little steps,
her hair is like hanging string,
her sight is dim,
she is so old she does not even go to the porch.
My wife's body has faded; she has no peace.
Her breasts are withered,
eaten and squeezed by the many children at her side.
In her misery, she plucks from the spinach plant on the heap
a young shoot not yet grown,
budding from a branch whose leaves were picked before,
she cooks it in saltless water,
she eats it with no buttermilk, with no rice.
The cloth she wears is short and dirty,
she who loves me,
who curses the justice of the world,
who never has enough to eat.
Your fame is such
that you can make both my mother and my wife happy,
giving like a cloud pouring down with lightning and roaring thunder
on millet that could not form its lovely, dark grain in the heat,
planted with rice on a broad field
burned over and plowed by forest men.
My whole family that now suffers from hunger
you could make happy.
Yet even if I receive a war elephant with high raised tusks,
I will not praise you, I will not accept that gift
if it is given grudgingly.
No, but if you give happily to delight me, sharp-speared Kumaṇaṉ,
I will take even a tiny crab's eye seed.
I who sing you ask this gracious act of you,

O lord of exalted fame,
born in a faultless line renowned for its victories.

Peruñcittiraṉār sings Kumaṇaṉ.

[Peruñcittiraṉār means "the great painter." Crab's eye seeds are scarlet, with black ends. They are very hard, often used in India for jewellers' weights. They are hollowed out and filled with tiny ivory elephants and then capped with an ivory plug to make a little toy often seen in the West. The crab's eye seed is about half the size of a pea.]

Puṟanāṉūṟu 160

"It was as if rain showered down
with thunder whose voice makes men tremble,
nourishing the forest
whose grass is burnt by the bright rays of the savage sun:
he gave rice and ghee and spicy meat
to cool our bowels, wrinkled, lined, and shrunken from lack of rice
until dried-up sweat coated our skin
and hunger withered our bodies.
Like the stars around the moon,
he had well-used dishes of gold placed around,
and saying,
'May the families of singers be without want,'
with ease he gave precious golden ornaments.
Such is Kumaṇaṉ,
who has the good fame of being closer to us than to his friends,
lord of Mutiram whose streets are filled with drink.
If you go to him, he will give you much."
With such words they praised you again and again,
and so, my heart urging me on, I came quickly.
My son, his topknot thin as a horse's plume,
is so tired of having nothing to eat in our house
he has forgotten he even has a home.
Again and again he sucks the milkless breast.
Frantically he opens one by one the empty containers
to get some rice or gruel,
and then he sobs.
To divert him,
his mother tells him an angry tiger is coming,
she shows him the moon,
she tells him to pretend he is angry at his father.
Lord, I ask you to give me right now much wealth
so that she who even in the day suffers pain
may know prosperity.

Then we will sing your great fame so it rises all over the earth
surrounded by the seas with breaking waves.

Peruñcittiraṉār sings Kumaṇaṉ.

[Children in ancient Tamilnad wore topknots. Even today, Tamil mothers show their children the moon, to stop their crying.]

Puṟanāṉūṟu 164

Our oven is never used for cooking,
its sides are not worn down,
toadstools grow on it.
My wife is thin from hunger.
Every time he sucks on her ugly, milkless breast,
its skin withered, its duct closed up,
our child sobs.
She sees his face,
and her cool, wet-lashed eyes fill with tears.
I saw her suffering,
thought of you, and came,
Kumaṇaṉ of good battle.
Now that you know my state,
I will not relent until you give,
even if I must force you,
for you were born in a line
that always met the needs of musicians,
whose good hide-covered lutes have strings tuned for each *rāga*,
whose drum heads are smeared with mud.

Peruntalaiccāttaṉār sings Kumaṇaṉ who, his kingdom taken by his younger brother, is living in the forest.

[This poem should be read with the next one.]

Puṟanāṉūṟu 165

Men who have wished for permanence in this impermanent world
have established their fame before they vanished.
Men of fabulous wealth,
unapproachable in their greatness,
have failed to be counted among the ancient ones
because they did not give to suppliants in need.
As I stood singing that king whose horses are swift,
whose good fame has no blemish,
who gives to singers war elephants
with decorated foreheads
and bells dangling down to their feet as they ring with each step,
he said,
"If a worthy suppliant leaves empty-handed,
it is worse than losing my kingdom,"
and he gave his sword and offered his head,
for he had nothing to give but himself.
With dancing and rejoicing I have come
having seen your lord, who always keeps his word.

Peruntalaiccāttaṉār, after seeing Kumaṇaṉ, whose kingdom had been taken by his younger brother and who was living in the forest, and after being given his sword, brought it, showed it to Iḷaṅkumaṇaṉ [Kumaṇaṉ's younger brother], and sang this song.

[Kumaṇaṉ is a fugitive, with a price on his head. His intention in offering his head is that at least Peruntalaiccāttaṉār can take it to his younger brother and collect a reward for it. The poet calls Kumaṇaṉ Iḷaṅkumaṇaṉ's lord because he is his elder brother. But he means to imply as well that he is a greater man.]

Puṟanāṉūṟu 182

This world exists only because
some men in it,
even when they might have the drink
that made the gods deathless,
will not drink it alone.
They do not hate or fail to act
even when they fear what others fear.
They will give their lives for fame
but they would not take even the entire earth
if it soiled their name.
They are never without joy,
and though they may be great,
they do not use their powers for themselves
but only for others.
Because of them this world is.

The song of Kaṭaluṇmāynta Iḷamperuvaḻuti.

[The poet's name means "Iḷamperuvaḻuti who perished [or disappeared] in the sea." From his title Vaḻuti, the poet must have been a Pandyan king or prince.]

Puṟanāṉūṟu 184

If ripe paddy is harvested
and made into food for an elephant,
then even a field smaller than a *mā*
gives enough for many days.
But if the elephant enters it alone,
even a field of a hundred *ceṟus* is useless,
the paddy will be trampled uneaten.
If a wise king taxes, aware of what is right,
his land can give a crore and flourish still.
But if a small man is king,
and is greedy to take, with no thought of kindness,
surrounded by men who do not know what is right,
who are loud in their praises,
then like the elephant that entered the field,
he will not eat and the world will perish.

The song of Picirāntaiyār when he went to Pāṇṭiyaṉ Aṟivuṭainampi.

[A *ceṟu* is about one and three-fourths acres. A *mā* is about one two thousandth of that. See the notes on Puṟanāṉūṟu 213 for the story of Picirāntaiyār. Even though one may infer from this poem that Pāṇṭiyaṉ Aṟivuṭainampi was not very considerate towards his subjects, he was a good enough poet to compose Puṟanāṉūṟu 188, which is one of the most famous poems in Tamil.]

Puṟanāṉūṟu 188

A man may have earned great riches,
he may eat with many,
he may have great wealth of possessions.
Yet if he has no children
who cover the ground with tiny steps as they walk,
who stretch out their little hands,
who put their food on the floor,
who smear their hands in it,
bite it, stir it,
and throw it,
delighting him as they cover themselves
with rice and ghee,
then all the days he lives
are worth nothing.

The song of Pāṇṭiyaṉ Aṟivuṭainampi.

Puṟanāṉūṟu 192

All lands home, all men kin.
Evil and good are not from others,
nor are pain and its abating.
Death is nothing new.
We do not rejoice thinking life sweet,
and if pain comes,
even less do we find it a cause for grief.
Through the eyes of those who see deeply
we have come to know that life takes its hard course
as if it were a raft in the waters of a mighty river,
ever roaring and beating on rocks
after cold rain pours from flashing skies,
and so we do not wonder at the great
and still less do we despise the small.

The song of Kaṇiyaṉ Pūṅkuṉṟaṉ.

[This is the most eloquent statement I know of the theory of *karma*, which holds that all actions bear fruit, either in this life or in some future life. The poet does not make a mechanistic statement of the theory of the sort that mars so much of Indian literature. Rather, he says that each person is responsible for what happens to him, but that this process is so hidden and mysterious that the only reasonable response is to treat all people with equanimity and compassion.]

Puṟanāṉūṟu 193

Like a deer driven by hunters
to a long salt flat as white
as a flayed hide spread upside down,
you might run and even escape
if living with family did not tie your feet.

The song of Ōrēruḻavar.

[See Kuṟuntokai 131, the poem from which the poet took his name.]

Puranāṉūṟu 213

In the thick of battle you show your strength,
your white umbrella shines, king of victories.
In this vast world, encircled by its roaring waters,
two men have risen against you.
They are not your old enemies with their established power,
they who come with hearts set on fighting.
You have nothing to gain through battle,
king whose elephants kill.
If you were to win fame by dying,
by going to paradise, where the great ones live,
what you leave behind would go to them.
You have a thirst for fame:
hear what I will say.
These young men who have risen against you
though firm in their resolve
have little judgment.
If they lose, to whom will you leave your wealth?
And if you lose, your enemies will be happy
and you will leave contempt behind you,
lord of furious battle.
Put down your weapons,
and, quickly rising, show your courage.
The shadow of your feet that helps the suffering
must not lose its fame.
You must do what is right.
You must become a guest
welcomed happily by the gods
in that world so hard for men to attain.

The song of Pullāṟṟūr Eyiṟṟiyaṉār to Kōpperuñcōḻaṉ, who was going [in battle] against his sons.

[This poem through Puṟanāṉūṟu 223 forms one of the most moving sequences in Tamil literature. The sequence tells of the death of

Kōpperuñcōḻaṉ, a great king whose two sons tried to take his throne by raising an army and coming against him. In this poem, the poet advises the king to give up the fight and to end his life in the rite of *vaṭakkiruttal*, in which a king faces north, with his sword at his side, and starves himself to death along with those closest to him. The king takes the advice of the poet, goes to a river islet, and, surrounded by his close friends, sits down to begin the rite. In the Pandyan kingdom to the south, there lived a great poet named Picirāntaiyār, who had never seen the Chola king but who considered him one of his best friends, having become acquainted with him by reputation and by the exchange of poems. In Poem 215, Kōpperuñcōḻaṉ expresses his anxiousness for the poet whom he has never seen to come and join him. Finally, Picirāntaiyār arrives, and Kōpperuñcōḻaṉ and his friends continue the rite. When they are dead, the places of their death are marked with the memorial stones erected to commemorate great heroes and to house their spirits.]

Puṟanāṉūṟu 215

Millet with forked stems,
pounded and boiled,
mixed with white yogurt
and white *vēḷai* flowers that budded on dung-filled streets—
all these are cooked in a tamarind sauce
by a cowherd woman
and fed to bean pickers until they are full
in the southern land of the Pandyan king,
where they say Piciröṉ lives.
I cannot die without him.
He may have stayed away in good times,
but he will not fail me now
that pain has come.

The words of Kōpperuñcōḻaṉ, telling the good men who said, "Picirāntaiyār will not come," "He will come."

[See the notes on Puṟanāṉūṟu 213. Picirōṉ is another name of Picirāntaiyār. It is a sign of prosperity for the street to be covered with powdered dung.]

Puṟanāṉūṟu 218

Gold, coral, pearls,
lovely sapphires given by a dark mountain—
these all come from far separate places,
and yet if they are strung
to make a priceless ornament
they stay together.
Always good men seek the company of the good,
evil men the company of evil.

The song of Kaṇṇakaṉār when he saw Picirāntaiyār facing north [to starve himself to death].

[See the notes on Puṟanāṉūṟu 213. This poem, which by itself is a bit commonplace, derives its effect from the circumstances under which it was sung.]

Puṟanāṉūṟu 219

On an island in a river,
in spotted shade,
you sit and your body dries up.
Are you angry with me, warrior
who have asked so many to join you here?

The song of Karuvūrp Peruñcatukkattup Pūtanātaṉār to Kōpperuñcōḻaṉ as he faced north [to starve himself to death].

[See the notes on Puṟanāṉūṟu 213. The poet is distressed that he was not asked by Kōpperuñcōḻaṉ to join him. River islets were sacred places in ancient Tamilnad. Today one of the greatest Indian temples, Śrīraṅgam, is on an islet in the Kāvēri river.]

Puṟanāṉūṟu 223

You gave shade to many,
the world praised you.
And yet you could not finish your reign
but had to reduce yourself to this small space,
where you have now become an undecaying stone.
And the other stones surely will be kind
and give me space,
for I come to them with an old love
that holds me to them
like life to the body.

Pottiyār, who has faced north [to starve himself to death] sings Kōpperuñcōḻaṉ who, even though he has become a stone, has given him a place [to sit].

[See the notes on Puṟanāṉūṟu 213. Perhaps the colophon means that Pottiyār, miraculously given permission to face north by the spirit of the dead king, asks the other memorial stones to make room for him.]

Puṟanāṉūṟu 228

In your large, old town,
your kiln spews thick smoke into the wide sky,
as black as gathered darkness.
Listen, potter, I pity you,
I do not know what you will do.
Great Vaḷavaṉ has gone to the world of the gods,
Vaḷavaṉ, who was born in the line of the Cempiyaṉs,
whose greatness
spreads as far as the broad rays of the sun in the sky,
its true fame praised by royal poets
whose vast armies cover the earth.
Now you must make an urn to hold him.
Do you think you can do it
with the earth for a wheel,
and a great mountain for your clay?

Aiyūr Muṭavaṉār sings Cōḻaṉ Kuḷamuṟṟattut Tuñciya Kiḷḷivaḷavaṉ.

[In ancient Tamilnad, corpses would either be cremated or excarnated and the bones collected and placed in urns.]

Puṟanāṉūṟu 232

May mornings and evenings stop coming,
may the days of my life be over.
On his stone
they place a peacock feather
and on it they pour filtered liquor.
Will he take it
who, when they offered him a whole country
with tall mountains and towering summits,
would not accept it?

Auvaiyār sings Atiyamāṉ Neṭumāṉ Añci.

[The stone is the memorial stone, which was thought to be inhabited by the spirit of a dead king or warrior.]

Puṟanāṉūṟu 235

If he had a little toddy, he would give it to us.
If he had much, he would drink it happily
as we sang and drank with him.
Whether the rice was scarce or abundant,
he would share it on many plates.
He would give us whole sides of meat and bones.
He would stand within range of spears and arrows.
His hand, fragrant with orange blossoms,
would stroke my head that stinks of flesh.
Before it fell to the ground,
the spear that went through his breast
made holes in the wide dishes of the best of bards;
it passed through the hands of suppliants;
and it pierced the tongues of poets with subtle skill at words,
dimming the pupils in the empty eyes of their families.
Where is my lord who was my support?
Now there are no singers,
and there are none who give to singers.
Like the dark *pakaṉṟai* flowers flowing with honey in a cool bay
that fade without ever being worn,
there are countless lives that pass
without giving anything to others.

Auvaiyār sings Atiyamāṉ Neṭumāṉ Añci.

[The old commentary explains that the king's hands are fragrant with orange blossoms because they give away so many garlands of that flower. At the end of each of the first six sentences, the Tamil has the word *maṉṉē*, whose meaning is something like "alas, it is no more."

Puṟanāṉūṟu 238

By the curved sides of a covered red urn,
a red-eared vulture and a *pokuval* bird sit without fear.
Crows with large beaks, horned owls, a band of demons
freely wander there.
Such is the wilderness he has gone to,
he who loved drink.
Ruined like the beauty now gone of his women
whose arms are bare of bangles,
the families of singers are miserable.
The heads of the royal drums are all torn.
Mountainlike elephants, driverless now, have lost their tusks.
Without knowing that my lord,
attacked by angry Death,
had suffered and died,
I came to him, and now I feel great pain.
What will happen to those who need me?
On a rainy night, when his boat has turned over,
heart bursting with agony,
a man eyeless and dumb sinks in the sea.
Rather than spinning like him
in a whirlpool of grief in a flood whose shore
cannot be known, whose waves tower,
death would be better and right.

The song of Peruñcittiraṉār after the death of Veḷimāṉ.

[The *pokuval* is some kind of bird of ill omen. The beginning of this poem describes the place where pots, filled with the bones of the dead, were put. See Puranāṉūṟu 159 for more on the poet Peruñcittiraṉār.]

Puṟanāṉūṟu 243

It is painful to remember.
By a cool pond, girls would play
picking flowers and putting them on dolls they made
with the firm sand.
I would hold their hands
and embrace them
and sway with them.
And then I and my friends,
still too young to lie or cheat,
would climb up on the branch
of a tall-limbed *marutam* tree growing near the water,
making it bend into the pond,
and as those on the shore looked on, afraid for us,
we would dive to the bottom of the deep water
and bring up handfuls of sand.
I was young then, when was it?
I support myself with a thick stick,
an ornament on its head,
I tremble;
coughing cuts short the few words I say.
I have grown very old.

The song of Toṭittalai Viḻuttaṇṭiṉār.

[The effect of this poem is achieved through the contrast of the sand with the gold ornament on the head of the cane.]

Puṟanāṉūṟu 245

Great it may be,
yet my grief has limits,
for it is not strong enough to kill me.
On the weed-strewn salt earth of the burning ground,
on a pile of logs set aflame
she lies,
her bed blazing fire.
My woman is dead, she belongs to the other world,
yet I am still alive.
This life is strange.

The song of Cēramāṉ Kōṭṭampalattut Tuñciya Mākkōtai, uttered upon the death of his principal wife.

Puranāṉūṟu 248

Surely this small white lily is to be pitied.
When we were young it made our dresses.
Now our lord who had great strength is dead,
and it gives us its seeds for our bland food,
eaten at the wrong times on days filled with pain.

The song of . . . Okkūr Mācāttaṉār.

[Widows were not supposed to eat rice, ghee, and other good-tasting food. Rather, as one of the restrictions they observed to keep their sexual powers under control, they were supposed to eat lily and bamboo seeds at the times of day when people normally did not eat. Other restrictions included tonsure, sleeping on a bed of stones, and wearing no ornaments. Young, chaste widows and the widows of high-born men often took their life in suttee.]

Pu<u>r</u>anā<u>n</u>ū<u>r</u>u 255

I would cry out for help, but I am afraid of tigers.
I would embrace you, but I cannot lift your broad chest.
May evil Death, who made you suffer so,
shiver as I do.
Take my wrist, thick with bangles,
and we will reach the shade of the mountain.
Come, walk, it is very near.

Va<u>n</u>paraṇar sings. . . .

[A woman addresses the body of her husband, who has been killed in battle. This poem is analyzed in the introduction.]

Puṟanāṉūṟu 256

Potter, you who make dishes, listen.
You should have pity on me,
for like a little white lizard on the spoke of a shafted wagon
I have crossed many barren places with him.
On this earth with its great expanses,
make the urn large enough for me too,
potter of this ancient, spacious town.

. . . .

[The widow asks the potter to make the urn large enough to contain her bones as well as her husband's. She means that she is about to take her own life.]

Puṟanāṉūṟu 271

In earth that has never known dryness
nocci grew with its dark clusters
until it furnished dresses
so bright they drew the eye
covering the loins of gentle, ornamented women.
But now we see a garland of *nocci*,
coated with blood,
transfigured,
hacked in pieces,
seized greedily by a vulture who thinks it meat,
because the man whose joy is fighting
wore it.

The song of Veṟipāṭiya Kāmakkaṇṇiyār.

[The author of this poem is a woman.]

Puranāṉūṟu 276

Her white hair unscented,
the nipples of her empty breasts wrinkled like *iravam* seeds,
she is the loving mother of a boy
who, like the few drops of curd an innocent cowherd girl
flicks with her strong nail into a pot of milk,
all alone spread suffering through a whole army.

The song of Maturaip Pūtaṉ Iḷanākaṉār.

[Just as it takes only a few drops of curd to turn a whole pot of milk into yogurt, it took only one man to rout the whole army.]

Puṟanāṉūṟu 278

Many said,
"That old woman, the one whose veins show
on her weak, dry arms where the flesh is hanging,
whose stomach is flat as a lotus leaf,
has a son who lost his nerve in battle and fled."
At that, she grew enraged and she said,
"If he has run away in the thick of battle,
I will cut off these breasts from which he sucked,"
and, sword in hand, she turned over fallen corpses,
groping her way on the red field.
Then she saw her son lying there in pieces
and she rejoiced more than the day she bore him.

The song of Kākkaipāṭiṉiyār Nacceḷḷaiyār.

[The author of this poem is a woman.]

Puranāṉūṟu 279

Her purpose is frightening, her spirit cruel.
That she comes from an ancient house is fitting, surely.
In the battle the day before yesterday,
her father attacked an elephant and died there on the field.
In the battle yesterday,
her husband faced a row of troops and fell.
And today,
she hears the battle drum,
and, eager beyond reason, gives him a spear in his hand,
wraps a white garment around him,
smears his dry tuft with oil,
and, having nothing but her one son,
"Go!" she says sending him to battle.

The song of Okkūr Mācāttiyār.

[A white garment is presented to a man before a great occasion even today in South India. And, even today, an oil bath is supposed to be initiated by one's mother, who smears a bit of oil on her son's head. The fact that the son still has a tuft shows that he is still a child.]

Puṟanāṉūṟu 281

Margosa and *iravam* with its sweet fruits have been placed around the house.
Behind the curved lute, many instruments sound.
With gentle hands, we will smear collyrium on his forehead;
we will scatter mustard seeds,
blow the flute,
strike musical bells,
sing songs of the transience of life,
and spread the fragrant smoke of incense through the house.
Come, friend, we will protect his wounds
whose feet wear anklets engraved with flowers,
who fought off the assault on the king.

The song of Aricilkiḻār.

[The various acts described in this poem are intended to protect the wounded man from dangerous sacred forces thought to threaten his life. The songs of the transience of life are called *kāñci*. Duraicami Pillai remarks, "Since the cause of all sickness is attachment, the *rāga* of *kāñci* was sung to cut attachment." Examples of *kāñci* in this collection are Puṟanāṉūṟu 349, 350, and 356.]

Puṟanāṉūṟu 300

"Bring me my shield," you say, "bring me my shield."
If you hide yourself behind a rock with your shield,
you might escape.
Yesterday you killed a man,
and today his younger brother,
his eyes rolling like crab's eye seeds in a wide-mouthed pot,
is looking for you
as if you were a jar of liquor brewed in a great city
and stored away in a house.

The song of Aricilkiḻār.

[See Puṟanāṉūṟu 159 for a description of a crab's eye seed. That the liquor was made in a great city means that it is especially fine.]

Puranāṉūṟu 305

A young Brahmin,
his waist thin as a *vayalai* creeper,
bowed and sad,
came to the camp at night,
entered without pausing,
and said a few words.
At that they gave up their ladders and stakes,
and bells were taken from the elephants of many wars.

The song of Maturaivēḷācāṉ.

[No one knows what the Brahmin said, but his words must have been powerful to have made one side abandon the war. Stakes were driven into the ground behind doors to keep them tightly closed in battle.]

Puṟanāṉūṟu 316

Again and again let us praise drink.
He who lies here in a stupor,
who got drunk this morning in this unswept, weed-filled courtyard,
is our king.
We are his bards.
Yesterday when guests arrived
he pawned the old sword at his side—
I will stake my small, black lute on the truth of it.
Do not think he will not give.
You too go to him,
and your woman,
her waist as thin as a creeper,
will put on a bright ornament,
and we, our glasses filled with drink, will be happy.
You too go to him and return,
with your mouth red from eating and drinking.
For today an enemy king with small-eyed elephants
has fallen before him in battle.

The song of Maturaik Kaḷḷiṟ Kaṭaiyattaṉ Veṇṇākaṉār.

[The poet means that his king, who yesterday was so poor that he had to pawn his sword to feed guests, is now rich from the booty taken from another king he killed in battle.]

Puṟanāṉūṟu 349

With the tip of his spear,
the king wipes the sweat from his forehead
and curses.
And her father curses back,
without one kind word to say.
Such is their state.
That lovely dark woman,
her teeth sharp,
her lined eyes cool and glistening,
like a little fire kindled in a tree,
has become a scourge to the city she was born in.

The song of Maturai Marutaṉ Iḷanākaṉār.

[This and the next poem describe the consequences of a lovely and high-born girl's attaining puberty. She becomes the object of desire of a king (or, as in the next poem, of kings), and when her people will not give her to him, he attacks her city to take her by force.]

Puṟanāṉūṟu 350

The moats are silted up,
the battlements weak,
the walls falling down.
What will become of our ancient town,
scarred as it is?
It cannot withstand a siege.
Their drums beating like thunder with falling rains,
their horses swift,
kings came in the morning
and roam about our towering gate.
Nor will her brothers be happy without a fight,
for they have the will and the strength to kill.
Her red eyes, blackened with collyrium,
seem sharp-bladed spears held high in the thick of battle.
Bangles slide on her young wrists.
And her lovely breasts are flushed with the spots of puberty.

The song of Maturaiyōlaikkaṭaik Kaṇṇampukuntārāyattaṉār

[See the notes on the preceding poem.]

Puṟanāṉūṟu 356

Overspread with salty soil,
overgrown with weeds,
where owls hoot in broad daylight
and demon women live whose mouths gape in the light of the pyres,
the burning ground spewing forth white clouds is fearful.
Their hearts full of desire, lovers weep
and their warm tears put out embers lying among the bones.
The burning ground has seen the back of every man,
for it alone is the end of all men on the earth.
No one has ever seen its back.

The song of Tāyaṅkaṇṇaṉār.

[To see a man's back in battle means that he is defeated and running away. Of course, the poet also has in mind the fact that the back of the corpse being cremated faces the earth.]

Puṟanāṉūṟu 363

Good-hearted kings who have ruled this great earth
surrounded by the black sea
so that not even a part of the center of one *uṭai* leaf
belonged to someone else—
even they have gone to the ground of burned corpses
as their final home,
more of them than there is sand heaped by the waves.
All have gone and perished, leaving their land to others.
That is why you too should listen.
There is no life which keeps an undying body.
Death is true, no illusion.
Before the ugly day
when on the wide burning ground
spread with milk-hedge and thorns and marked with rising biers,
a man of despised birth takes boiled, saltless rice
and gives it to you turning away from your face
so that you eat an unwanted sacrifice whose vessel is the earth,
do what you have planned
and give up the earth utterly, whose boundary is the sea.

Aiyāticciṟu Veṇṭēraiyār sings. . . .

[The poet evidently counsels the king to become an ascetic. He makes his point well by describing the earth as the container for the sacrifice offered to the dead corpse. Death is so horrible that even the untouchable is unwilling to look the corpse in the face. *Uṭai* is the umbrella thorn, a small tree with white flowers and very tiny leaflets.]

Puṟanāṉūṟu 364

The poetess puts on an unwithering garland
and the bard's head shines with a fire-brilliant lotus
that never flowered in a pond.
We will put a black goat on the fire and eat.
With our tongues we will push juicy pieces of spiced meat
around our mouths that are red from drink.
And we will feed suppliants.
Come, let us rejoice, you of fierce battle!
These things will be hard to enjoy, lord,
the day we go to the ground of burial urns
where male owls cry out ceaselessly
from the hollows of ancient trees
whose many roots,
fallen so they split the earth,
sway in the wind.

Kūkaikkōḻiyār sings. . . .

[The poet's name means "he of the male owl." In Kuṟ. 393, given above, Paraṇar has borrowed his image. The lotus flower at the beginning of the poem is made of gold.]

FURTHER READING

Basham, L. *The Wonder that was India*. New York, Evergreen, 1961. This book contains a short but well-written account of Tamil literature before the Muslim invasion.

Hart, George L., III. *The Poems of Ancient Tamil: Their Milieu and Their Sanskrit Counterparts*. Berkeley, University of California Press, 1975.

Ilango Adigal. *Shilappadikaram (The Ankle Bracelet)*. Translated by A. Danielou. New York, New Directions, 1965. As poetry, this translation of the fifth-century Tamil work is quite good. It is, however, not as accurate as one could wish.

———. *The Silappadikaram*. Translated by V. R. Ramachandra Dikshitar. Madras, Oxford University Press, 1939. This translation is more accurate and scholarly than Danielou's, but it is less poetic.

C. and H. Jesudasan. *A History of Tamil Literature*. Calcutta, Y.M.C.A. Publishing House, 1961.

Kailasapathy, K. *Tamil Heroic Poetry*. London, Oxford University Press, 1968.

Le Paripāṭal. Translated into French and annotated by François Gros. Pondichéry, Institut Français d'Indologie, 1968. This is a good French translation of one of the anthologies.

Pope, G. U. *The Naladiyar, or Four Hundred Quatrains in Tamil*. Oxford, Clarendon Press, 1893. This is a Victorian translation of an ancient Tamil ethical work that dates back to perhaps the fourth century A.D.

———. *The Tiruvacagam or "Sacred Utterances" of the Tamil Poet, Saint, and Sage Manikka-vacagar*. Oxford, Clarendon Press, 1900. This translation of medieval Tamil devotional hymns is valuable for its notes, remarks, and introduction rather than for the translation, which lacks accuracy and is stilted.

Ramanujan, A. K. *The Interior Landscape, Love Poems from a Classical Tamil Anthology*. Bloomington, Indiana, Indiana University Press, 1967. This short book contains excellent translations from the *Kuṟuntokai*.

———. *Speaking of Siva*. Baltimore, Penguin Books, 1973. This is a selection of medieval devotional poems from Kannada, a sister language of Tamil. The translations are fine, and the material important for anyone interested in Dravidian India.

Thani Nayagam, Xavier S. *Landscape and Poetry. A Study of Nature in Classical Tamil Poetry*. Bombay, Asia Publishing House, 1965.

Vaiyapuri Pillai, S. *History of Tamil Language and Literature*. Madras, New Century Book House, 1956. Vaiyapuri Pillai invariably gives dates for texts that are too late.

Zvelebil, Kamil. *The Smile of Murugan: On Tamil Literature of South India*. Leiden, E. J. Brill, 1973.

———. *Tamil Literature*. Leiden, E. J. Brill (Handbuch der Orientalistik, zweite Abteilung, 2 Band, 1 Abschnitt), 1975.

———. *Tamil Literature*. Wiesbaden, Otto Harrassowitz (A History of Indian Literature, Vol. I), 1974. Each of these three volumes by Zvelebil contains material on the anthologies. The first and third of these books contain more analysis and interpretation than the second, which is intended as a handbook, giving mostly facts.

LIBRARY OF CONGRESS CATALOGING IN PUBLICATION DATA

Main entry under title:

Poets of the Tamil anthologies.

(Princeton library of Asian translations)
Bibliography: p.
CONTENTS: Ainkuṟunūṟu.—Kuṟuntokai.—Naṟṟiṇai.—
Akanāṉūṟu.—[etc.]
1. Tamil poetry—To 1500—Translations into English.
2. English poetry—Translations from Tamil. I. Hart,
George L. II. Series.
PL4762.E3P6 894'.811'11 79-83993
ISBN 0-691-06406-7

GPSR Authorized Representative: Easy Access System Europe - Mustamäe tee 50, 10621 Tallinn, Estonia, gpsr.requests@easproject.com

www.ingramcontent.com/pod-product-compliance
Lightning Source LLC
Chambersburg PA
CBHW050633300426
44112CB00012B/1777
9780691608457